The Healthy Smoothie Recipe Book for Beginners

500 Delicious Smoothies

RECIPES TO LOSE WEIGHT, GAIN ENERGY AND DETOX

Anthony Green

The information in this book is not intended as medical advice or to replace a one-on-one relationship with a qualified health care professional. It is intended as a sharing of knowledge and information from the research and experience of Anthony Green. We encourage you to make your own health care decisions based on your research and in partnership with a qualified health care professional. You may not be familiar with many of the ingredients listed herein. To help, we've included some basic information for many of the more unusual items. However, please note that some of the ingredients are considered medicinal in nature. So, before consuming large quantities of anything you're not familiar with (or, if you have any special medical condition or are taking any prescription medication), please do a bit of research and/or talk to a medical professional when in doubt.

Anthony Green

INTRODUCTION	8
HOW TO USE THIS BOOK	9
WHAT HAPPENS TO YOUR BODY WHEN YOU DRINK A SMOOTHIE EVERY DAY	10
Helps You Lose Weight	*11*
You could get an easy boost of protein.	*11*
Prevents Dehydration	*11*
Makes You Feel Full	*11*
Aid In Digestion	*11*
Source of Antioxidants	*12*
Enhances Immunity	*12*
Curbs Sleep Disorders	*12*
Improves Skin	*12*
Provides Liquid Food Benefits	*12*
Detoxifies the Body	*12*
Boosts Brain Power	*13*
Controls Mood Swings	*13*
Fights Depression	*13*
Supplies Calcium	*13*
Checks the Growth of Carcinogens	*13*
Provides a Good Amount of Fiber	*13*
Improves Bone Health	*14*
Prevents Heart Disorders	*14*
Reduces Chances of Cancer	*14*
Balances Hormonal Functioning	*14*
Your blood sugar may spike.	*14*
BONUS TIPS	15
You might still feel hungry after.	*15*
You might go over your calorie target for the day.	*15*
Organic & seasonal	*16*
Preparation	*16*
Breakfast Sweet Smoothies	*17*
Lunch Smoothies	*17*
Dinner Green Smoothies	*18*
RECIPES	19
BREAKFAST SMOOTHIES	20
PEACH BLUEBERRY SMOOTHIE	21
PEACHES AND CREAM OATMEAL SMOOTHIE	21
HONEYDEW MELON AND KIWIFRUIT SMOOTHIE	21
ORANGE AND YOGURT SMOOTHIE	21
PEANUT BUTTER & JELLY SMOOTHIE	21
PEACH OAT SMOOTHIE	21
MIXED-BERRY BREAKFAST SMOOTHIE	21
COCONUT BLUEBERRY SMOOTHIE	21
PUMPKIN PIE SMOOTHIE	22
FRUIT & YOGURT SMOOTHIE	22
STRAWBERRY & BANANA ALMOND SMOOTHIE	22
SUPER BERRY SMOOTHIE	22
TWO-MINUTE BREAKFAST SMOOTHIE	22
BREAKFAST SMOOTHIE	22
TROPICAL BREAKFAST SMOOTHIE	22
HEALTHY MUESLI BANANA BREAKFAST SMOOTHIE	23
STRAWBERRY OATMEAL BREAKFAST SMOOTHIE	23
OATMEAL SMOOTHIE	23
GREEK YOGURT SMOOTHIE	23
WATERMELON SMOOTHIE	23
HAWAIIAN BERRY SMOOTHIE	23
BERRY LAYER	24
STRAWBERRIES & CREAM	24
CHOC MINT SMOOTHIE	24
BERRY SMOOTHIE	24
COLLAGEN BOOST SMOOTHIE	24
TRIPLE CHOCOLATE MOCHA SMOOTHIE	24
PUHOI VALLEY CARAMEL AND WHITE CHOCOLATE SMOOTHIE	24
PASSIONFRUIT VANILLA AND CHIA SEED SMOOTHIE	24
ALL-BERRY SMOOTHIE	25
HOT CHOCOLATE SMOOTHIE	25
APPLE PIE SMOOTHIE	25
GINGERBREAD SPICE SMOOTHIE	25
SKINNY MINT SMOOTHIE	25
EPIC ALMOND SMOOTHIE	25
CHOCOLATE WEIGHT LOSS SMOOTHIE	26
BERRY, CHIA, AND MINT SMOOTHIE	26
BERRY-ALMOND SMOOTHIE	26
BANANA CREAM PIE SMOOTHIE	26
TRIPLE BERRY SMOOTHIES	26
PINEAPPLE COCONUT MANGO SMOOTHIE	26
VERY BERRY SMOOTHIE	26
EASY STRAWBERRY PINEAPPLE SMOOTHIE	27
PEACH & OATMEAL SMOOTHIE	27
KEY LIME PIE SMOOTHIE	27
FRUITY POWER SMOOTHIE	27
MANGO RASPBERRY SUNSHINE YOGURT SMOOTHIE	27
AWBERRY MANGO PEACH SMOOTHIE	27
TROPICAL SMOOTHIE	28
WILD BLUEBERRY POMEGRANATE SMOOTHIE	28
BANANA ALMOND FLAX SMOOTHIE	28
CINNAMON BUN BREAKFAST SMOOTHIE	28
STRAWBERRY COCONUT OAT SMOOTHIE	28
PEACH & OAT BREAKFAST SMOOTHIE	28
CABBAGE AND BERRY PURPLE SMOOTHIE	28
STRAWBERRY BANANA OAT SMOOTHIE	29
CRANBERRY POMEGRANATE SMOOTHIE	29
PUMPKIN CHEESECAKE BREAKFAST SMOOTHIE	29
BANANA BERRY SMOOTHIES	29
RASPBERRY BANANA SMOOTHIES	29
PINA COLADA OAT BREAKFAST SMOOTHIES	29
PAPAYA MANGO SMOOTHIE WITH LEMON AND GINGER	29
PAPAYA BANANA SMOOTHIE WITH PEANUT BUTTER	30
GUAVA SMOOTHIE WITH STRAWBERRIES AND BANANA	30
CREAMY DRAGON FRUIT SMOOTHIE	30
BLUEBERRY PAPAYA SMOOTHIE	30
TANGY BAOBAB SUNSHINE SMOOTHIE	30
SUPERFOOD BLUEBERRY SPINACH SMOOTHIE	30
RASPBERRY PEACH SMOOTHIE	30

PEACH COBBLER SMOOTHIE	31
APPLE CIDER VINEGAR	31
FRUIT & YOGURT SMOOTHIE	31
UNICORN SMOOTHIE	31
PERFECT BERRY SMOOTHIE	31
PERFECT STRAWBERRY SMOOTHIE	31
CHIA SEED SMOOTHIE	31
PERFECT BANANA SMOOTHIE	31
CHOCOLATE BLACK BEAN SMOOTHIE	32
AMAZING APPLE CINNAMON WEIGHT GAIN SMOOTHIE	32
MATCHA KIWI NICE SMOOTHIE	32
PINK MERMAID SMOOTHIE	32
COTTON CANDY SMOOTHIE	32
PURPLE SMOOTHIE	32
BERRY GINGER SMOOTHIE	32
SALTED CARAMEL SMOOTHIE	32
BERRY KIWI YOGURT SMOOTHIE	32
APPLE BERRY YOGURT SMOOTHIE	33
PEANUT BUTTER BANANA OATMEAL SMOOTHIE	33
MANGO PEACH AND STRAWBERRY SMOOTHIE	33
BERRY BANANA BREAKFAST SMOOTHIE	33
SKINNY ORANGE DREAM BREAKFAST SMOOTHIE	33
CHOCOLATE, BANANA AND ALMOND BUTTER BREAKFAST SMOOTHIES	33
BANANA OATMEAL BREAKFAST SMOOTHIE	33
STRAWBERRY BANANA BREAKFAST SMOOTHIE	33
CHOCOLATE BANANA BREAKFAST SMOOTHIE	34
BERRY GREEN BREAKFAST SMOOTHIE	34
STRAWBERRY BLUEBERRY CHIA SMOOTHIE	34
GINGERBREAD SMOOTHIE	34
PEACH WITH OAT SMOOTHIE	34
MATCHA SMOOTHIE	34
PEACH SMOOTHIE	34
CARAMEL SMOOTHIE	34
ALMOND BUTTER SMOOTHIES	35

DETOX SMOOTHIES 36

CREAMY KALE SMOOTHIE	37
ANTIOXIDANT BERRY AVOCADO SMOOTHIE	37
APPLE SMOOTHIE	37
GREEN SMOOTHIE	37
BERRY SMOOTHIE	37
LIVER SMOOTHIE	37
5-INGREDIENT SMOOTHIE	37
PINEAPPLE-GRAPEFRUIT SMOOTHIE	38
VITAMIX TRIPLE BERRY SMOOTHIE	38
APPLE PIE SMOOTHIE	38
MORE VITAMIX SMOOTHIE	38
VITAMIX BANANA RASPBERRY GREEN SMOOTHIE	38
BEET POMEGRANATE CITRUS SMOOTHIE	38
DETOX SMOOTHIE	38
LEMON KALE PROTEIN	38
ENERGIZING ANTIOXIDANT SMOOTHIE	39
ISLAND GREEN SMOOTHIE	39
SUPERFOOD GREEN DETOX SMOOTHIE	39
DELICIOUS ARUGULA SMOOTHIE	39
SWEETIE PEA GREEN SMOOTHIE	39
GREEN PROTEIN SMOOTHIE	39
GLOWING GREEN SMOOTHIE	39
APPLE BERRY SMOOTHIE	40
PINEAPPLE BANANA SMOOTHIE	40
PEACHES AND CREAM OATMEAL GREEN SMOOTHIE	40
BERRY DELICIOUS DETOX DIET SMOOTHIE	40
KALE AND APPLE GREEN SMOOTHIE	40
KALE PINEAPPLE COCONUT SMOOTHIE	40
KALE STRAWBERRY BANANA SMOOTHIE	40
AVOCADO DETOX SMOOTHIE	40
LIVER DETOX GREEN SMOOTHIE	41
BEETROOT SMOOTHIE	41
METABOLISM BOOSTING BLUEBERRY SMOOTHIE	41
EASY DETOX SMOOTHIE	41
EASY FLAX SEED SMOOTHIE	41
DETOX JUICE	41
SPIRULINA SMOOTHIE	41
BLUEBERRY DETOX SMOOTHIE	41
APPLE, SPINACH, AND LIME SMOOTHIE	42
BEST BEET SMOOTHIE	42
BROCCOLI DETOX SMOOTHIE	42
BROCCOLI LEMON DETOX SMOOTHIE	42
CELERA SMOOTHIE	42
BEST GREEN SMOOTHIE	42
5-MINUTE SMOOTHIE	42
SIRTUIN GREEN DETOX SMOOTHIE	43
DETOX SIRT SMOOTHIE	43
TROPICAL ISLAND GREEN SMOOTHIE	43
GREEN DETOX CUCUMBER SMOOTHIE	43
PINEAPPLE AND CUCUMBER DETOX SMOOTHIE	43
BLUEBERRY LIMON DETOX SMOOTHIE	43
SPINACH CUCUMBER SMOOTHIE	43
DETOX CARROT & TURMERIC SMOOTHIE	43
KALE SMOOTHIE	44
GREEN DETOX KETO SMOOTHIE	44
PURPLE POWER DETOX SMOOTHIE	44
GREEN DETOX SMOOTHIE FOR A HEALTHIER BREAKFAST	44
GOLDEN DETOX SMOOTHIE	44
MIXED BERRY DETOX SMOOTHIE	44
GREEN MIX DETOX SMOOTHIE	44
CLEANSE & DETOX SMOOTHIE	45
NATURALLY SWEET GREEN DETOX JUICE	45
DETOX SPINACH GREEN SMOOTHIE	45
TURMERIC PERSIMMON SMOOTHIE {VEGAN}	45
VEGAN PROBIOTIC BERRY SMOOTHIE	45
ANTIOXIDANT BLACKBERRY KALE SMOOTHIE {VEGAN}	45
SUPER GREEN AVOCADO SMOOTHIE	45
AIP GREEN DETOX SMOOTHIE	45
AIP TROPICAL SMOOTHIE	46
GREEN APPLE DETOX SMOOTHIE	46
HYDRATING PARSLEY DETOX SMOOTHIE	46
CHLORELLA DETOX SMOOTHIE	46
LIME SMOOTHIE	46
SUPER FOOD SMOOTHIE	46

CHERRY SMOOTHIE	46
CHERRY BEET SMOOTHIE FOR DETOX AND GUT HEALTH	47
CRANBERRY CHERRY SMOOTHIE	47
SOUR CHERRY AND POMEGRANATE DETOX SMOOTHIE	47
PINEAPPLE DETOX SMOOTHIE	47
WATERMELON DETOX WATER RECIPE	47
MANGO SMOOTHIE	47
MANGO GREEN TEA DETOX SMOOTHIE	47
PINEAPPLE MANGO DETOX SMOOTHIE	47
MANGO BANANA CELERY DETOX SMOOTHIE	48
MANGO GINGER DETOX SMOOTHIE	48
SPRING CLEANING MANGO DETOX SMOOTHIE	48
SKIN DETOX GREEN SMOOTHIE	48
MANGO LIME GREEN SMOOTHIE	48
DETOX GLOWING SKIN SMOOTHIE	48
KIWI DETOX SMOOTHIE	48
SPRING DETOX - SMOOTHIE	49
SUPER ENERGY DETOX SMOOTHIE	49
ULTIMATE GREEN DETOX SMOOTHIE (DAIRY FREE, VEGAN)	49
GREEN APPLE CUCUMBER DETOX SMOOTHIE	49
CRANBERRY APPLE DETOX SMOOTHIE	49
LOW CARB CUCUMBER GREEN TEA DETOX SMOOTHIE	49
CLEANSE & DETOX SMOOTHIE: DAIRY, SUGAR & GLUTEN FREE	49
BLUEBERRY BANANA DETOX SMOOTHIE	50
GRAPEFRUIT DETOX SMOOTHIE	50
HEALTHY GRAPEFRUIT GINGER DETOX SMOOTHIE	50
GRAPEFRUIT, STRAWBERRY & SPINACH DETOX SMOOTHIE	50

green smoothie — 51

SMOOTHIE WITH BANANA AND HONEY ON MILK	52
MILK AND HONEY SMOOTHIE	52
STRAWBERRY-BANANA GREEN SMOOTHIE	52
GREEN PINEAPPLE COCONUT SMOOTHIE	52
SPINACH, PEANUT BUTTER & BANANA SMOOTHIE	52
SPINACH-AVOCADO SMOOTHIE	52
PINEAPPLE GREEN SMOOTHIE	52
MANGO & SPINACH SMOOTHIE	52
TROPICAL GREEN SMOOTHIE	53
REALLY GREEN SMOOTHIE	53
JASON MRAZ'S AVOCADO GREEN SMOOTHIE	53
GOOD GREEN TEA SMOOTHIE	53
GREEN PINA COLADA SMOOTHIE	53
ALL GREENS SMOOTHIE	53
SPINACH SMOOTHIE	53
3-INGREDIENT TROPICAL GREENS SMOOTHIE	53
PINEAPPLE SPINACH SMOOTHIE	54
GREEN SMOOTHIE	54
STRAWBERRY GREEN GODDESS SMOOTHIE	54
CLEANSING APPLE AVOCADO SMOOTHIE	54
ALKALINE VEGETABLES SMOOTHIE CUBES	54
PINEAPPLE GINGER SMOOTHIE	54
ISLAND GREEN SMOOTHIE	54
KALE RECHARGE SMOOTHIE	54
SPRIG OF PARSLEY	55
GREEN CINNAMON SMOOTHIE	55
STRAWBERRY SPINACH GREEN SMOOTHIE	55
MANGO GREEN TEA SMOOTHIE	55
COLD BUSTER GREEN SMOOTHIE	55
AVOCADO GREEN SMOOTHIE	55
KALE AND KIWI GREEN SMOOTHIE	55
AVOCOLADA SMOOTHIE	56
MAGIC BROCCOLI SMOOTHIE	56
BEST KALE SMOOTHIE	56
PERFECT CELERY SMOOTHIE	56
EASY CUCUMBER SMOOTHIE	56
GLOWING GREEN SMOOTHIE	56
PERFECT AVOCADO SMOOTHIE	56
BEST SPINACH SMOOTHIE	57
GLOWING GREEN BANAN SMOOTHIE	57
CREAMY GREEN SMOOTHIE	57
GREEN BREAKFAST SMOOTHIE	57
PINEAPPLE AVOCADO GREEN SMOOTHIE	57
BANANA MATCHA SMOOTHIE	57
MANGO MATCHA GREEN TEA SMOOTHIE	57
IRON RICH TROPICAL GREEN SMOOTHIE	58
HEALTHY MANGO SPINACH SMOOTHIE	58
REFRESHING KALE APPLE SMOOTHIE	58
TROPICAL MATCHA SMOOTHIE	58
MORNING GREEN SMOOTHIE	58
KALE PINEAPPLE SMOOTHIE	58
PISTACHIO SMOOTHIE	58
FROZEN SPINACH SMOOTHIE WITH GINGER ROOT	59
PINEAPPLE AND CUCUMBER SMOOTHIE FOR WEIGHT LOSS	59
AVOCOLADA KALE TROPICAL SMOOTHIE	59
BROCCOLI SMOOTHIE	59
GREEN CHIA SMOOTHIE	59
GLOWING GREEN CHIA SMOOTHIE	59
CREAMY GREEN CHIA SMOOTHIE	59
BASIC GREEN SMOOTHIE	60
GREEN MONSTER SMOOTHIE	60
GREEN KIWI SMOOTHIE	60
KALE & PINEAPPLE SMOOTHIE	60
BRAIN FOOD SMOOTHIE	60
ROMAINE AROUND SMOOTHIE	60
TEA FOR ONE SMOOTHIE	60
BEST GREEN SMOOTHIE	61
HOW TO MAKE A SMOOTHIE	61
AVOCADO APPLE GREEN SMOOTHIE	61
SCRUB YOURSELF CLEAN GREEN SMOOTHIE	61
METABOLISM BOOSTING GREEN SMOOTHIE	61
STRAWBERRY BANANA GREEN SMOOTHIE	61
APPLE PIE GREEN SMOOTHIE	61
ELECTRIC GREEN BOOST SMOOTHIE	61
CRISP MANGO CUCUMBER GREEN SMOOTHIE	62
GREEN TROPICAL SUNRISE	62
CRAZY FOR KALE	62
TROPICAL GREEN COCONUT MILK SMOOTHIE	62
RASPBERRY-BANANA GREEN SMOOTHIE	62
WEIGHT LOSS GREEN SMOOTHIE	62
CHIA BERRY GREEN PROTEIN SMOOTHIE	62

FOOD PROCESSOR SMOOTHIE	62
SPIRULINA SMOOTHIE	63
IRON RICH SMOOTHIE	63
GREEN APPLE SMOOTHIE	63
BROCCOLI SMOOTHIE WITH PINEAPPLE	63
COLLARD GREENS SMOOTHIE	63
AWESOME AVOCADO AND BANANA SMOOTHIE	63
KETO AVOCADO SMOOTHIE	63
FAVORITE GREEN SMOOTHIE	64
ENERGIZING MATCHA SMOOTHIE	64
SHAMROCK SMOOTHIE	64
BROCCOLI SPROUT SMOOTHIE	64
SPINACH ALMOND SMOOTHIE	64
CREAMY ZUCCHINI SMOOTHIE	64
KALE AND GINGER SMOOTHIE	64
SPINACH ALMOND SMOOTHIE	65
DANDELION AND WATERCRESS SMOOTHIE	65

smoothie recipes for weight loss _____ 66

LEAN, MEAN, GREEN MACHINE	67
BANANA ALMOND PROTEIN SMOOTHIE	67
WORKOUT RECOVERY SMOOTHIE	67
PROTEIN POWER SMOOTHIE	67
PEACH OAT SMOOTHIE	67
DOUBLE CHOCOLATE MINT SMOOTHIE	67
COCONUT ALMOND SMOOTHIE	67
BLUEBERRY BREAKFAST SMOOTHIE	67
BERRY-COCONUT SMOOTHIE	68
MATCHA MADNESS SMOOTHIE	68
BLUE BOMB SMOOTHIE	68
MANGO-ALMOND SMOOTHIE	68
BERRY BLAST PROTEIN SMOOTHIE	68
FRUIT SMOOTHIE	68
VANILLA MATCHA SMOOTHIE	68
GRAPEFRUIT SMOOTHIE	69
TROPICAL SMOOTHIE	69
SAVORY TOMATO SMOOTHIE	69
EASY FLAXSEED SMOOTHIE	69
GRAPEFRUIT SMOOTHIE	69
DRAGON FRUIT SMOOTHIE	69
HONEY TURMERIC SMOOTHIE	69
PEACH SMOOTHIE	69
SUMMER WATERMELON SMOOTHIE	70
CHERRY ACAÍ SMOOTHIE	70
PCOS SMOOTHIE	70
PERFECT LEMON SMOOTHIE	70
HEALTHY PINEAPPLE SMOOTHIE	70
WEIGHT GAIN SMOOTHIE	70
HEALTHY BLUEBERRY SMOOTHIE	70
IMMUNE BOOSTING SMOOTHIE	70
RASPBERRY CHOCOLATE SMOOTHIE	71
COCONUT CASHEW PROTEIN SMOOTHIE	71
POMEGRANATE AND BERRY HIGH-PROTEIN SMOOTHIE	71
COFFEE PROTEIN SMOOTHIE	71
STRAWBERRY PROTEIN	71
STRAWBERRY PROTEIN SMOOTHIE	71
VANILLA PROTEIN SMOOTHIE	71
MANGO SMOOTHIE WITH YOGURT	71
CITRUS KIWI SMOOTHIE	72
PEAR SMOOTHIE	72
COCONUT OIL SMOOTHIE	72
FRUIT AND VEGETABLE SMOOTHIE	72
SLEEP WELL SMOOTHIE	72
CHOCOLATE PROTEIN SMOOTHIE	72
RED BERRY PROTEIN SMOOTHIE	72
PROTEIN SMOOTHIE	73
OATMEAL PROTEIN SMOOTHIE	73
SNICKERDOODLE PROTEIN SMOOTHIE	73
MORNING SMOOTHIE	73
ALMOND BUTTER & BANANA PROTEIN SMOOTHIE	73
BERRY SPINACH PROTEIN SMOOTHIE	73
FOR HEALTHY PROTEIN SMOOTHIES	74
PINA COLADA SMOOTHIE	74
HIGH PROTEIN BLUEBERRY KALE SMOOTHIE	74
BANANA OATMEAL SMOOTHIE	74
CREAMY BLACKBERRY SMOOTHIE	74
HOLIDAY CRANBERRY SMOOTHIE	74
CINNAMON DATE SMOOTHIE	74
FAT BURNING SMOOTHIE FOR WEIGHT LOSS	74
CHOCOLATE PEANUT BUTTER SMOOTHIE	75
DARK CHOCOLATE BANANA NUT	75
AB OF STEEL	75
BLACK AND BLUE BERRY VANILLA PROTEIN SMOOTHIE	75
SUPER THICK BLUEBERRY SMOOTHIE	75
CHOCOLATE DECADENCE	75
TABASCO CHERRY	75
ORANGE CREAMSICLE SMOOTHIE	76
ALMOND GINGER BLUEBERRY ANTI-INFLAMMATORY SMOOTHIE	76
PEACH OAT SMOOTHIE	76
CHOCOLATE BEET SMOOTHIE	76
ANTI INFLAMMATORY BERRY GINGER SMOOTHIE	76
POWER BREAKFAST SMOOTHIE	76
BLUEBERRY SMOOTHIE	76
STICKY DATE SMOOTHIE	77
MEAL REPLACEMENT SMOOTHIE	77
OAT AND BERRY SMOOTHIE	77
MANGO SMOOTHIE	77
HEMP CAT	77
WARM CHAI SMOOTHIE	77
CHERRY SMOOTHIE	77
VEGAN BREAKFAST SMOOTHIE	78
PEANUT BUTTER BANANA SMOOTHIE	78
FIESTA SAVORY SMOOTHIE	78
CREAMY BANANA SMOOTHIE	78
BUTTERNUT SQUASH SMOOTHIE	78
CREAMY AVOCADO SMOOTHIE	78
ALMOND BUTTER SMOOTHIE	78
ORANGE JULIUS SMOOTHIE	79
SMOOTHIE FOR BLOATING	79
SUMMER MELON SMOOTHIE	79

ADRENAL FATIGUE DIET SMOOTHIE	79
BEST GREEN PROTEIN SMOOTHIE	79
MCT OIL SMOOTHIE	79
CHERRY BEET SMOOTHIE	79
GREEN ENERGY SMOOTHIE	79
BLUEBERRY CHIA SMOOTHIE	80
APPLE CELERY SMOOTHIE	80
STRAWBERRY OAT SMOOTHIE	80
WATERMELON MINT SMOOTHIE	80
ANTI-INFLAMMATORY CHERRY-SPINACH SMOOTHIE	80
MANGO RASPBERRY SMOOTHIE	80
CARROT-APPLE SMOOTHIE	80
CITRUS-PINEAPPLE SMOOTHIE	81
BLUEBERRY & AVOCADO SMOOTHIE	81
STRAWBERRY-MANGO-BANANA SMOOTHIE	81
CRANBERRY AND RASPBERRY SMOOTHIE	81
HIGH IN VITAMIN C	81
BERRY-KEFIR SMOOTHIE	81
MANGO COLADA SMOOTHIE	81
PINEAPPLE BANANA SMOOTHIE	81
SMOOTHIE FOR PREGNANCY	82
PEACH RASPBERRY SMOOTHIE	82
PUMPKIN SMOOTHIE	82
MOJITO SMOOTHIE	82
COCONUT MILK SMOOTHIE	82
EASY BEET SMOOTHIE	82
BEST ALMOND MILK SMOOTHIE	82
BEST PEANUT BUTTER SMOOTHIE	82
CARROT SMOOTHIE	83
NUTRIENT-DENSE SMOOTHIE	83
BAHAMA MAMA SMOOTHIE	83
MATCHA BANANA SMOOTHIE	83
STRAWBERRY BLUEBERRY SMOOTHIE	83
VEGAN PUMPKIN PIE SMOOTHIE	83
STONE FRUIT SMOOTHIE	83
SWEET POTATO SMOOTHIE	84
BERRY FENNEL SMOOTHIE	84
FENNEL FROND AND PINEAPPLE SMOOTHIE	84
POMELO SMOOTHIE	84
BLUEBERRY SMOOTHIE	84
CARROT APPLE SMOOTHIE WITH GINGER	84
EASY BERRY POMEGRANATE SMOOTHIE	84
TROPICAL JACKFRUIT SMOOTHIE	84
CREAMY APPLE STRAWBERRY SMOOTHIE	85
SIMPLE STRAWBERRY OAT MILK LACTATION SMOOTHIE	85
POST WORKOUT SMOOTHIE	85
EASY MANGO SMOOTHIE	85
ACTIVATED CHARCOAL SMOOTHIE	85
KIWI BERRY SMOOTHIE	85
BERRY YOGURT SMOOTHIE	85
BLACKBERRY ACTIVATED CHARCOAL SMOOTHIE	85
CHIA BANANA BOOST SMOOTHIE	86
COPYCAT CARIBBEAN PASSION SMOOTHIE	86
PINEAPPLE SMOOTHIE	86
RASPBERRY AND APPLE SMOOTHIE	86
STRAWBERRY KIWI SMOOTHIE	86
LOW CALORIE SMOOTHIES	86
AVOCADO & STRAWBERRY SMOOTHIE	86
KIWI FRUIT SMOOTHIE	86
BANANA, CLEMENTINE & MANGO SMOOTHIE	87
AVOCADO & BANANA SMOOTHIE	87
COCONUT JOY VEGAN SMOOTHIE	87
BRAIN FOG CURE SMOOTHIE	87
RASPBERRY LEMON SMOOTHIE	87
VEGAN RASPBERRY PEANUT BUTTER SMOOTHIE	87
CHERRY COLLAGEN SMOOTHIE	87
SAUERKRAUT JUICE SMOOTHIE	87
ELECTROLYTE RECOVERY SMOOTHIE	88
PURPLE PASSION GREEN SMOOTHIE	88
MOCHA SMOOTHIE WITH COCONUT MILK	88
PINEAPPLE COCONUT MILK SMOOTHIES	88
HEALTHY MIXED BERRY SMOOTHIE	88
PEANUT BUTTER BANANA COCONUT MILK SMOOTHIE	88
STRAWBERRY COCONUT MILK SMOOTHIE	88
STRAWBERRY BANANA COCONUT MILK SMOOTHIE	88
CHOCOLATE CHERRY ANTI-INFLAMMATORY SMOOTHIE	88
MEAL REPLACEMENT SMOOTHIE FOR WEIGHT LOSS	89
MIXED BERRY COCONUT MILK SMOOTHIES	89
VANILLA PEACH COCONUT MILK SMOOTHIE	89
LOW CARB SMOOTHIE	89
LOW CALORIE PAPAYA SMOOTHIES	89
WEIGHT LOSS COLLAGEN SMOOTHIE	89
RED VELVET SMOOTHIE	89
BERRY ORANGE SMOOTHIE	89
STRAWBERRY BANANA SMOOTHIE	90
BANANA BLUEBERRY AND SPINACH SMOOTHIE	90
OCEAN SMOOTHIE	90
ULTIMATE BANANA NICE CREAM	90
BANANA, HONEY & HAZELNUT SMOOTHIE	90
ANTI-CANCER GREEN SMOOTHIE	90
OAT MILK SMOOTHIE WITH STRAWBERRY AND BANANA	90
PEANUT BUTTER SMOOTHIE	90
BLACKBERRY SMOOTHIE	91
MORINGA SMOOTHIE	91
AVOCADO CHOCOLATE SMOOTHIE (VEGAN)	91
ZUCCHINI STRAWBERRY SMOOTHIE	91
VEGAN STRAWBERRY CHEESECAKE SMOOTHIE	91
MANGO STRAWBERRY BANANA SMOOTHIE	91
PEANUT BUTTER CAULIFLOWER SMOOTHIE	91
STRAWBERRY BEET CONSTIPATION SMOOTHIE	91
HONEYDEW SMOOTHIE	92
SWISS CHARD SMOOTHIE	92
BERRY SMOOTHIE	92
FROZEN FRUIT SMOOTHIE	92

Introduction

If you are looking for rich, fast and healthy food that energizes your body, smoothies are the perfect solution! Made with fruits and vegetables, they contain lots of vitamins and fibre that will keep your body happy and help you stay productive throughout the day. And they taste amazing too!

There's nothing like a cold smoothie to kickstart your morning on a refreshing note, keep those hunger pangs at bay between meals, or re-fuel right after a grueling workout. Smoothies are very helpful for improving your digestive system, immune system, maintain your blood sugar, cholesterol level, blood flow, and definitely for weight loss. All the smoothies in this book also give you enough energy, which is necessary for your body.

Smoothie Cleanses are all the rage right now. Nutribullets and blenders are selling like hot cakes, and it is common to see people walking down the street sipping on brightly colored drinks. Well, now you can join them and take the first step to achieving extraordinary health! For some, a smoothie is a beloved part of their daily routine—and it makes sense when you consider their convenience: You can quickly whip one up before heading out the door to run errands, or grab one on the way to the work to power you through those morning meetings.

The beauty of a smoothie lies in the endless possibilities: You can incorporate whatever fruits or veggies you like, and then customize the blend to fit your needs at the moment with add-ins like protein powder, seeds, nut butter, or whole grains. That means that how healthy your smoothie habit is will depend largely on the ingredients you include.

That said, there are a number of clear health benefits—and risks—to sipping on a smoothie daily. Here's what you need to know before you fire up that blender.

Anthony Green

HOW TO USE THIS BOOK

Smoothies do not cure illnesses, but they can contribute physically and psychologically to the process of self-healing. The recipes in this book have been created with specific, common health issues in mind—things my clients regularly come to see me about—but I also want this book to act as a guide to motivate you towards better general health.

The recipes here are good for everyone and can be enjoyed at any time, with food or as a snack. The smoothies can be enjoyed instead of a meal if you have a busy day—it's better to have a smoothie than have nothing to eat and end up starving! You can follow the fast days from time to time and, if you have an ailment, use the recipes specific to your health concern. However, with or without health issues, juices and smoothies are a fantastic way to get a real boost of goodness with minimal effort.

Some drinks are stronger tasting than others, so if you are just starting out, use the recipes that have a higher fruit content, especially berries, and then move on to other ones. You will be surprised how fast you get used to the different tastes. Some of the recipes have unusual ingredients, but most ingredients can be found either in supermarkets or in health food stores.

I hope you will grow in confidence and knowledge and learn how to substitute an ingredient for something similar that is easier.

What Happens to Your Body When You Drink a Smoothie Every Day

HELPS YOU LOSE WEIGHT

Smoothies can help you lose excess body weight without skipping any meals. The fruits and berries that are used to prepare these drinks serve as excellent companions for keeping you healthy and feeling cooler on a hot summer morning. The enzymes present in several fruits help dissolve body fat and clear up your circulatory system.

YOU COULD GET AN EASY BOOST OF PROTEIN.

The average vegetable only has about 2.5 grams of protein per serving. But if you add other ingredients—say, a tablespoon of almond butter or hemp seeds—you can boost the protein by a significant amount.

I suggest adding a clean, high-quality protein powder to complement your daily needs, especially if you're physically active three or more days a week, or trying to build muscle. Greek yogurt is an excellent source of protein to add to your smoothies—and as an added bonus, it'll make your blends a whole lot creamier, too. In order to cut down on the sugar content, opt for unsweetened Greek yogurt rather than the flavored kinds.

PREVENTS DEHYDRATION

Water is the most abundant thing both on earth and in your body. About 70 percent of your body is water. Having smoothies along with breakfast is a great way to replenish the loss of water in your body during the summer.

MAKES YOU FEEL FULL

People trying to lose weight often skip the morning meal and end up snacking on food in larger amounts between meals. To avoid this, experts advise having smoothies made of excellent fruits and flavors so that you stay full for a long time.

AID IN DIGESTION

Green smoothies that contain a lot of green leafy vegetables add essential vitamins and minerals to breakfast and aid in digestion. The fiber supplied by these drinks multiplies the benefits of having a delicious breakfast, especially during the summer.

SOURCE OF ANTIOXIDANTS

Green tea is a popular source of antioxidants. You can add matcha green tea powder to make your smoothies rich in antioxidants, and these will help prevent a lot of diseases. Grapes, berries and sweet potatoes are natural sources of antioxidants.

ENHANCES IMMUNITY

Immunity refers to the ability of your body to fight against pathogens and diseases. This natural potential becomes degenerated due to several reasons. Interestingly, having smoothies made of ingredients that include nutrients like beta-carotene helps boost your immune system.

CURBS SLEEP DISORDERS

People belonging to different age groups around the world often face issues related to lack of sleep and restlessness. A healthy breakfast accompanied by a smoothie made of bananas, kiwi and oats provides calcium and magnesium in good amounts. This induces sleep and helps maintain healthy sleeping patterns.

IMPROVES SKIN

As you may know, food containing carotenoids, like mango and pumpkin, are highly beneficial for skin and complexion. Therefore, smoothies that contain these ingredients help you keep glowing in the summer.

PROVIDES LIQUID FOOD BENEFITS

Health and nutrition experts worldwide suggest consuming liquid food for better digestion. Smoothies contain blended fruits and vegetables in liquid form that make it easier for the body to break them down.

DETOXIFIES THE BODY

Foods like garlic, papaya and beets help cleanse your blood and get rid of several toxins accumulated in your body tissues. Thus to have a great breakfast you should include smoothies as reliable detoxifying drinks every day.

BOOSTS BRAIN POWER

It is quite evident that that certain fruits and vegetables increase brain power and boost memory. Mental alertness and concentration is greatly enhanced by ingredients like coconut that are rich in omega-3 fatty acids. Smoothies with these ingredients help the brain work faster.

CONTROLS MOOD SWINGS

Organic fruits and vegetables serve as excellent stress busters. Smoothies made of fresh ingredients relieve stress and help you stay happier and healthier.

FIGHTS DEPRESSION

Fresh vegetables and fruits that are rich in folic acid, like broccoli, spinach and bananas, help keep depression at bay. Patients suffering from depression are advised to eat healthy breakfasts, and smoothies can be very helpful for them.

SUPPLIES CALCIUM

A regular intake of calcium in the right amount is essential for bone and tooth health. Moreover, it can affect hair growth and heart functioning too. Smoothies prepared with dairy or fortified dairy alternatives serve as great sources of calcium for the body.

CHECKS THE GROWTH OF CARCINOGENS

The growth of cancer-causing factors, or carcinogens, can be checked by controlling the growth of free radicals in the body. Fruits like strawberries, blueberries and grapes are rich in antioxidants that inhibit the growth of cancer-causing free radicals.

PROVIDES A GOOD AMOUNT OF FIBER

The most common problem people suffer from today is related to upset bowels. A good amount of fibrous food is essential for regulating the excretory system so that you can enjoy summer without worrying about your health. Smoothies with a lot of fruits and vegetables help keep your bowels functioning smoothly.

IMPROVES BONE HEALTH

Calcium, vitamin D3 and vitamin K are nutrients that improve bone health. Smoothies rich in these nutrients contain spinach, green vegetables and citrus fruits as chief ingredients. So for the best breakfast, you should try some cool smoothies that ensure your bones stay healthy forever.

PREVENTS HEART DISORDERS

Coronary diseases, or ailments related to heart, require nutrient-rich food along with appropriate medication. Timely breakfast that contains fat-free foods like oats and smoothies accompanied by regular exercising is the key for patients wishing to keep away from heart disorders.

REDUCES CHANCES OF CANCER

Several health reports published worldwide suggest that foods like cabbage, broccoli, and cauliflower are helpful in fighting against cancer. They attack free radicals and thus prevent cancer. Smoothies made of these ingredients prove really helpful in preventing cancer growth.

BALANCES HORMONAL FUNCTIONING

Hormones play a large role in regulating our day-to-day functions. However, any imbalance in their respective levels can lead to grave repercussions. Moreover, a hormonal imbalance can invite several health hazards. Therefore, to keep your hormones working smoothly, all you need is a refreshing smoothie of your choice. This will make you feel cool and calm this summer.

YOUR BLOOD SUGAR MAY SPIKE.

Without a doubt, the main drawback of drinking smoothies on the regular is that they're often loaded with sugar.This is especially true of bottled store-bought smoothies since they often contain added syrups to enhance the flavor.
Fortunately, if you make your smoothie at home, you can minimize the amount of sugar by reaching for ingredients like whole fruit (rather than sweetened juice) and unflavored yogurt. I recommend using water or unsweetened non-dairy milk to reduce the sugar content and overall calories in your smoothie.

BONUS TIPS

YOU MIGHT STILL FEEL HUNGRY AFTER.

Speaking of the sweet stuff, did you know that it causes spikes and drops in your blood sugar that can actually make you feel hungry? Not only that but since you're liquifying the fruits and vegetables, you're missing out on some of the fiber, which is what makes food satiating.
Smoothies are bypassing an important part of the digestive process which is mastication or chewing, foods are therefore absorbed more rapidly—so you may be hungrier a lot faster depending on what ingredients you are using.
I advise incorporating a protein and/or fiber source if you drink a smoothie every day so your stomach won't be rumbling an hour after you finish it. Since fiber fills you up, too, i suggest chia seeds or ground flaxseeds, which can add some texture to your smoothie while also making it more filling.
Always remember that a smoothie is not meant to replace every single meal in your day, but rather be used as a complement to your diet. If you are going to use it as a meal replacer, ensure that it packs all the components of a healthy meal (Protein, fruits/veggies, and whole grains).

YOU MIGHT GO OVER YOUR CALORIE TARGET FOR THE DAY.

A smoothie can quickly become a secret calorie bomb, especially once you start adding calorie-dense foods like dried fruit. So, keep in mind that it is possible to add too much of a good thing—even when it comes to healthy fat sources like peanut butter, avocado, and shredded coconut.
Be careful with nuts, nut butter, and seeds. You may add these options but remember they pack a lot of calories in small amounts.
Because it can be easy to go overboard if you're just eyeballing the amounts, consider measuring these ingredients out with a tablespoon.
There's one rule to abide by if you want to make your smoothie as healthy as possible: always make it yourself. When you blend it up at home, you have more control over not only the specific ingredients but also the portion sizes of each. A daily smoothie can offer a super convenient way to get your fruits and veggies in while also nourishing your body with many essential vitamins and minerals. The key is to maximize those benefits by focusing on whole, nutrient-dense foods while avoiding added sugars as much as possible.

ORGANIC & SEASONAL

I always use organic, if I can, to avoid pesticides. It means that there is no need to peel the produce first (unless using something like a mango, avocado, or papaya), just rinse and you are ready to go. Organic produce can be much more expensive and is not always available, so if this is the case, you might need a little more preparation.

For non-organic ingredients, peel what can be peeled and give everything a thorough wash because pesticides are persistent. You'll need to be ultra-careful in your washing, especially with leaves. Lettuce and spinach are among the most contaminated vegetables because they suck up pesticides from the soil and are sprayed the most to prevent the little bugs that love them.

Some ingredients are very seasonal, and if they aren't in season but still on the supermarket shelves, then they may be expensive and it will have taken a lot of air miles to get them there. This is when frozen foods are great. You can get all sorts of organic and non-organic fruits in the freezer section, picked and frozen right away, which preserves their nutrients. Frozen berries or peaches are great in smoothies and juices, and you could also try frozen summer leaves like spinach and spring greens. So you see, there is never an excuse to not eat a rainbow of fruits and vegetables every day!

PREPARATION

I tend not to core anything, but I do remove pits from any fruits that need it. Your juicer and blender will not thank you for putting a plum pit through them. If you use a juicer with a large chute, you shouldn't need to cut anything up. A little tip for juicing small leaves like rosemary is to wrap them in bigger leaves, and pass them through the juicer that way. For smoothies, I core and cube anything that requires it. Peel things like avocados, mangoes, and papaya, basically anything with a tough skin.

As I have said, if it is organic you can get away with not peeling, but I would advise you to peel non-organic produce. It is the quickest and easiest way to remove any pesticides that have been used.

For citrus fruits, I prefer to use a citrus press rather than put peeled citrus fruits through the juicer. You can also squeeze the fruit by hand.

BREAKFAST SWEET SMOOTHIES

A nutritious breakfast smoothie gives a good start to your day. It gives you the energy to keep going all day long. In the summer, people around the world look for ways to blend flavor and good nutrition together and get relief from the scorching heat. Having smoothies with breakfast every day can surely pave the way for good health and enjoyment throughout the hot season.

It also prevents dehydration: Water is the most abundant thing both on earth and in your body. About 70 percent of your body is water. Having breakfast smoothies is a great way to replenish the loss of water in your body during the summer.

Detoxifies your body
Foods like garlic, papaya, and beets help cleanse your blood and get rid of several toxins accumulated in your body tissues. Thus, to have a great breakfast you should include smoothies as reliable detoxifying drinks every day.

Keeps Blood Sugar in Check
High blood sugar and diabetes are the most common lifestyle diseases that bother people all around the world. People who have imbalanced sugar levels in their blood are prone to several complications. Thus having a breakfast that is rich in nutrients but low in calories can make things easier.

LUNCH SMOOTHIES

Makes you feel full: People trying to lose weight often skip the morning meal and end up snacking on food in larger amounts between meals. To avoid this, experts advise having smoothies made of excellent fruits and flavors so that you stay full for a long time.

Controls Cravings
Smoothies are full of nutrients and flavor. They are an essential part of the best luches, as they provide a power-packed start for the day. A lot of protein along with many nutrients subdue food cravings and keep you away from eating junk food.

Boosts Brain Power
It is quite evident that certain fruits and vegetables increase brain power and boost memory. Mental alertness and concentration is greatly enhanced by ingredients like coconut that are rich in omega-3 fatty acids. Smoothies with these ingredients help the brain work faster.

DINNER GREEN SMOOTHIES

Health and nutrition experts worldwide suggest consuming liquid food for better digestion. Smoothies contain blended fruits and vegetables in liquid form that make it easier for the body to break them down.

Curbs Better Digestion

People belonging to different age groups around the world often face issues related to lack of sleep and restlessness. A healthy dinner accompanied by a smoothie made of bananas, kiwi, and oats provides calcium and magnesium in good amounts. This induces sleep and helps maintain healthy sleeping patterns.

Aid in Digestion

Green smoothies that contain a lot of green leafy vegetables add essential vitamins and minerals to dinner and aid in digestion. The fiber supplied by these drinks multiplies the benefits of having a delicious dinner smoothie, especially during the summer.

Provides a Good Amount of Fiber

The most common problem people suffer from today is related to upset bowels. A good amount of fibrous food is essential for regulating the excretory system so that you can enjoy summer without worrying about your health. Smoothies with a lot of fruits and vegetables help keep your bowels functioning smoothly.

RECIPES

BREAKFAST SMOOTHIES

PEACH BLUEBERRY SMOOTHIE

Nutrition: Cal 170; Fat 4 g; Carb 26 g; Protein 8.5 g
Serving 1; Cook time 10 min

Ingredients
- 1 cup chilled almond or vanilla soy milk
- 1 slices of fresh or frozen peaches (about 1/2 cup)
- 1/2 cup blueberries, a handful of kale
- 1/2 tsp. ground cinnamon

Instructions
1. In a blender, combine all the ingredients and blend until smooth.

PEACHES AND CREAM OATMEAL SMOOTHIE

Nutrition: Cal 283; Fat 3.5 g; Carb 53.5 g; Protein 13g
Serving 1; Cook time 15 min

Ingredients
- 1 cup whole milk
- 1/2 cup Greek yogurt
- 1/2 cup rolled oats
- 1 cup frozen banana
- 1/2 frozen peaches
- 1/2 cup ice until smooth

Instructions
1. In a blender, combine all the ingredients and blend until smooth.

HONEYDEW MELON AND KIWIFRUIT SMOOTHIE

Nutrition: Cal 285; Fat 1 g; Carb 51 g; Protein 19 g
Serving 1; Cook time 15 min

Ingredients
- 1 cup honeydew melon chunks
- 1/2 cup plain non-fat Greek yogurt
- 1/2 cup non-fat milk
- 1 kiwi fruit, peeled and sliced
- 1 tablespoon honey
- 1/2 teaspoon cinnamon
- 1/2 cup ice

Instructions
1. In a blender, combine all the ingredients and blend until smooth.

ORANGE AND YOGURT SMOOTHIE

Nutrition: Cal 239; Fat 1 g; Carb 44 g; Protein 18 g
Serving 1; Cook time 15 min

Ingredients
- 1/2 cup non-fat milk
- 1/2 cup non-fat Greek yogurt
- 1/2 cup rolled oats
- 1 tablespoon honey
- 1/4 teaspoon vanilla extract
- 1/2 cup ice

Instructions
1. In a blender, combine all the ingredients and blend until smooth

PEANUT BUTTER & JELLY SMOOTHIE

Nutrition: Cal 367; Fat 10,9 g; Carb 7,1 g; Protein 53,9 g
Serving 1; Cook time 15 min

Ingredients
- 1 cup coarsely chopped kale
- 1 1/2 cup frozen pineapple chunks
- 1/2 cup plain Greek yogurt
- 1/2 cup unsweetened almond milk
- 1 tsp honey

Instructions
1. In a blender, combine all the ingredients and blend until smooth

PEACH OAT SMOOTHIE

Nutrition: Cal 142; Fat 3 g; Carb 28 g; Protein 4 g
Serving 1; Cook time 10 min

Ingredients
- 2 ripe peaches (quartered, pits removed*)
- 1 Tbsp chia seeds
- 1/4 cup rolled oats (gluten-free for GF eaters)
- 1/2 frozen banana (peeled before freezing)
- 1/4 cup fresh orange juice
- 1/2 cup low - fat milk
- 1/3 cup non- fat plain Greek yogurt
- 1 cup baby spinach
- 1 cup frozen banana slices (about 1 medium banana)
- 1/2 cup frozen strawberries
- 1 tablespoon natural peanut butter
- 1-2 teaspoons pure maple syrup or honey (optional)

Instructions
1. Add milk and yogurt to a blender, then add spinach, banana, strawberries, peanut butter and sweetener (if using); blend until smooth.

MIXED-BERRY BREAKFAST SMOOTHIE

Nutrition: Cal 424; Fat 21 g; Carb 55 g; Protein 17 g
Serving 1; Cook time 10 min

Ingredients
- 1 cup frozen mixed berries
- 3/4 cup water
- 1/2 cup low-fat plain Greek yogurt
- 1 banana
- 1/4 avocado
- 2 tablespoons chopped walnuts

Instructions
1. Combine berries, water, yogurt, banana, avocado and walnuts In a blender.
2. Blend on high speed until smooth.
3. If necessary, add more water to reach desired consistency.

COCONUT BLUEBERRY SMOOTHIE

Nutrition: Cal 283; Fat 11,3 g; Carb 46,5 g; Protein 1,5 g
Serving 1; Cook time 10 min

Ingredients
- 1/4 cup light coconut milk

- 1/4 cup orange juice
- 2 tablespoons coconut cream
- 1 cup frozen blueberries
- 1 tablespoon maple syrup (Optional)

Instructions
1. Add all ingredients to a blender and let set for 5-10 minutes so the oats and chia seeds can soak. Then blend until smooth

PUMPKIN PIE SMOOTHIE

Nutrition: Cal 247; Fat 6,1 g; Carb 41,9 g; Protein 10,2 g
Serving 1; Cook time 10 min

Ingredients
- 1 medium frozen banana
- 1/2 cup unsweetened almond milk or other nut milk
- 1/3 cup plain whole-milk Greek yogurt
- 1/3 cup canned pumpkin puree
- 1/8 teaspoon pumpkin pie spice
- 1-2 teaspoons pure maple syrup

Instructions
1. Place banana, almond milk (or other nut milk), yogurt, pumpkin puree, pumpkin pie spice and maple syrup in a blender. Blend until smooth.

FRUIT & YOGURT SMOOTHIE

Nutrition: Cal 283; Fat 3 g; Carb 46,5 g; Protein 1,5 g
Serving 1; Cook time 10 min

Ingredients
- 3/4 cup nonfat plain yogurt
- 1/2 cup 100% pure fruit juice
- 1/2 cups (6 1/2 ounces) frozen fruit, such as blueberries, raspberries, pineapple or peaches

Instructions
1. Puree yogurt with juice in a blender until smooth. With the motor running, add fruit through the hole in the lid and continue to puree until smooth.

STRAWBERRY & BANANA ALMOND SMOOTHIE

Nutrition: Cal 373; Fat 17 g; Carb 36 g; Protein 17 g
Serving 1; Cook time 10 min

Ingredients
- 1 small banana,
- 7 strawberries, hulled
- 3 tbsp 0% bio-yogurt
- 2 tbsp ground almond

Instructions
1. Slice the banana into the bowl of a food processor, or a jug if using a hand blender. Add the strawberries, yogurt, milk and ground almonds, and blitz until completely smooth. Pour into a glass and enjoy.

SUPER BERRY SMOOTHIE

Nutrition: Cal 117; Fat 1 g; Carb 18 g; Protein 8 g
Serving 1; Cook time 10 min

Ingredients
- 2 tsp honey (optional)
- 1 cup bag frozen berry
- 1 cup pot fat-free strawberry yogurt
- 1 cup milk
- ½ cup porridge oat

Instructions
1. Whizz the berries, yogurt and milk together with a stick blender until smooth. Stir through the porridge oats, then pour into 4 glasses and serve with a drizzle of honey, if you like.

TWO-MINUTE BREAKFAST SMOOTHIE

Nutrition: Cal 156; Fat 3 g; Carb 25 g; Protein 4 g
Serving 1; Cook time 10 min

Ingredients
- 1 banana
- 1 tbsp porridge oats
- 80g soft fruit (whatever you have – strawberries, blueberries, and mango all work well)
- 1 cup milk
- 1 tsp honey
- 1 tsp vanilla extract

Instructions
1. Put all the ingredients in a blender and whizz for 1 min until smooth.
2. Pour the banana oat smoothie into two glasses to serve.

BREAKFAST SMOOTHIE

Nutrition: Cal 124; Fat 1 g; Carb 25 g; Protein 2 g
Serving 2; Cook time 5 min

Ingredients
- 1 small ripe banana
- 1/2 cup blackberries, blueberries, raspberries or strawberries (or use a mix), plus extra to serve
- apple juice or mineral water, optional
- runny honey, to serve

Instructions
1. Slice the banana into your blender or food and add the berries of your choice. Whizz until smooth. With the blades whirring, pour in juice or water to make the consistency you like.
2. Toss a few extra fruits on top, drizzle with honey and serve.

TROPICAL BREAKFAST SMOOTHIE

Nutrition: Cal 189; Fat 1 g; Carb 38 g; Protein 4 g
Serving 2; Cook time 10 min

Ingredients
- 3 passion fruits
- 1 banana, chopped
- 1 small mango, peeled, stoned and chopped
- 1 cup orange juice
- ice cubes

Instructions
1. Scoop the pulp of the passion fruits into a blender and add the banana, mango and orange juice. Purée until smooth and drink immediately, topped with ice cubes.

HEALTHY MUESLI BANANA BREAKFAST SMOOTHIE

Nutrition: Cal 274; Fat 3 g; Carb 53 g; Protein 11 g
Serving 2; Cook time 10 min

Ingredients
- 1 cup Low Fat Milk
- 3/4 cup Low Fat Yogurt
- 1/4 cup Muesli
- 2 medium Bananas (sliced and frozen)
- 1/2 teaspoon Ground Cinnamon
- 2 teaspoons Pure Maple Syrup or Honey
- 1 teaspoon Vanilla Extract

Instructions
1. Place all the ingredients in a high-speed blender and blend until smooth.
2. Pour in serving glasses and enjoy immediately.

STRAWBERRY OATMEAL BREAKFAST SMOOTHIE

Nutrition: Cal 254; Fat 3 g; Carb 56 g; Protein 5 g
Serving 2; Cook time 10 min

Ingredients
- 1/2 rolled oats
- 1 almond milk
- 1 large banana, sliced and frozen
- 14 strawberries, frozen
- 2 tablespoons honey, maple syrup, or agave

Instructions
1. Add the oats to a blender and pulse a few times until the oats are finer.
2. Add the milk, banana, strawberries, and honey, and blend until smooth and combined.

OATMEAL SMOOTHIE

Nutrition: Cal 327; Fat 11 g; Carb 54 g; Protein 8 g
Serving 1; Cook time 10 min

Ingredients
- 1/4 cup old-fashioned oats or quick oats
- 1 banana chopped into chunks and frozen
- 1/2 cup unsweetened almond milk
- 1 tablespoon creamy peanut butter
- 1/2 tablespoon pure maple syrup plus additional to taste
- 1/2 teaspoon pure vanilla extract
- 1/2 teaspoon ground cinnamon
- 1/8 teaspoon kosher salt

Instructions
1. Place the oats in the bottom of a blender and pulse a few times until finely ground. Add the banana, milk, peanut butter, maple syrup, vanilla, cinnamon, and salt.
2. Blend until smooth and creamy, stopping to scrape down the blender as needed. Taste and add additional sweetener if you'd like a sweeter smoothie. Enjoy immediately.

GREEK YOGURT SMOOTHIE

Nutrition: Cal 392; Fat 10 g; Carb 57 g; Protein 25 g
Serving 1; Cook time 10 min

Ingredients
- 1 cup whole frozen strawberries about 10 large berries or mixed berries of choice
- 1 medium ripe banana peeled and cut in half
- 3/4 cup nonfat plain Greek yogurt
- 2 tablespoons oatmeal
- 1 tablespoon peanut butter or almond butter
- 1 to 2 teaspoons honey
- Water or unsweetened almond milk as needed
- Ice

Instructions
1. Place all of the ingredients but the ice in a blender: strawberries, banana, Greek yogurt, oatmeal, peanut butter, and 1 teaspoon honey.
2. Blend until smooth.
3. Depending upon the size and power of your blender, you may need to stop it and scrape down the pitcher a couple of times.
4. If the mixture is too thick to blend, splash in a little water or almond milk, stir to move the contents of the blender around, and blend again; if it is too thin, blend in a few ice cubes. Taste and add additional honey if you would like the smoothie sweeter.

WATERMELON SMOOTHIE

Nutrition: Cal 157; Fat 1 g; Carb 35 g; Protein 7 g
Serving 1; Cook time 10 min

Ingredients
- 3 cups 1-inch diced frozen watermelon cubes
- 1 cup frozen strawberries
- 1/2 cup vanilla Greek yogurt see notes to make vegan/dairy free
- 1/2 tablespoon honey plus additional to taste; see notes to make vegan
- 1/2 cup water or unsweetened almond milk as needed to blend
- 1/4 cup packed fresh mint leaves

Instructions
1. Place all of the ingredients in a high-powered blender: watermelon, strawberries, yogurt, honey, water, and mint.
2. Blend until smooth, adding more water as needed if the smoothie is too thick.
3. Taste and add additional honey if you'd like the smoothie sweeter (this will vary depending upon your brand of yogurt and preferences).

HAWAIIAN BERRY SMOOTHIE

Nutrition: Cal 288; Fat 3 g; Carb 66 g; Protein 6 g
Serving 1; Cook time 10 min

Ingredients
- 1 orange, sliced
- 2 frozen bananas, sliced
- 1 cup frozen mango
- 1/4 cup orange juice, plus more if smoothie is too thick

Instructions
1. In a blender, combine all the ingredients and blend until smooth.

BERRY LAYER

Nutrition: Cal 288; Fat 3 g; Carb 66 g; Protein 6 g
Serving 1; Cook time 10 min

Ingredients
- 1 container berry yogurt, roughly 5.3-6 oz
- 2 cups frozen berries, strawberries, blackberries
- 1 frozen banana, sliced
- ¼ cup milk, plus more if smoothie is too thick

Instructions
1. In a blender, combine all the ingredients and blend until smooth.

STRAWBERRIES & CREAM

Nutrition: Cal 240; Fat 6 g; Carb 35 g; Protein 17
Serving 1; Cook time 10 min

Ingredients
- ½ cup frozen strawberries
- 1 banana
- ¼ cup yoghurt of your choice
- Handful of cashew nuts
- Milk of your choice

Instructions
1. Place all of your chosen smoothie ingredients into a blender, then blend with enough milk to reach your desired consistency.

CHOC MINT SMOOTHIE

Nutrition: Cal 270; Fat 12 g; Carb 28 g; Protein 8
Serving 1; Cook time 10 min

Ingredients
- 1 cup Milk of your choice – we used regular cows milk
- 1/4 1/2 cup Water
- 1 ripe Banana (or half a large one) – frozen
- 1/2 Avocado – just ripe
- 3 tablespoons Wholegrain Rolled Oats
- 1 tablespoon Chia Seeds
- 1/2 1 teaspoon Peppermint Essence

Instructions
1. Place all ingredients in blender and blitz until smooth. Start with less peppermint essence and add more if needed, according to your taste.

BERRY SMOOTHIE

Nutrition: 354 cal, 9 g pro, 69 g carb, 8 g fiber, 7 g fat
Serving 1; Cook time 10 min

Ingredients
- 1 cup frozen mixed berries/blueberries
- 1 banana
- ½ cup acidophilus yoghurt
- 1 tsp honey (optional)

Instructions
1. Place any bananas that are going to go brown before you get a chance to eat them into the freezer to use in future for this recipe. Simply peel, break into bite sized chunks and place into a labeled plastic bag before placing into the freezer.

COLLAGEN BOOST SMOOTHIE

Nutrition: Cal 121; Fat 2 g; Carb 25 g; Protein 2 g
Serving 1; Cook time 10 min

Ingredients
- 1/2 -1 frozen banana
- 1 frozen cucumber
- 1/4 avocado
- 1 bsp LSA
- 1/2 cup milk of choice
- 1 packet collagen

Instructions
1. Combine banana, cucumber, avocado, LSA, milk and collagen in a blender until smooth.
2. Top with berries, banana, coconut flakes and seeds.

TRIPLE CHOCOLATE MOCHA SMOOTHIE

Nutrition: Cal 246; Fat 3 g; Carb 31 g; Protein 4 g
Serving 1; Cook time 10 min

Ingredients
- 1 cup almond milk - chocolate (can substitute if desired)
- 1 banana
- 1 row (4 pieces) dark chocolate
- 2 ice cubes
- 1 double espresso using Hummingbird Oomph Espresso
- 2 scoops chocolate ice cream dairy free

Instructions
1. Blend all ingredients together and top with roughly chopped chocolate (optional).

PUHOI VALLEY CARAMEL AND WHITE CHOCOLATE SMOOTHIE

Nutrition: Cal 336; Fat 13 g; Carb 28 g; Protein 11 g
Serving 1; Cook time 10 min

Ingredients
- 3 x 300ml bottles Puhoi Valley Caramel & White Chocolate Milk, well chilled
- 8 raw cashew nuts, roughly chopped
- 6 raw almonds, roughly chopped
- 3 ready to eat dates, pitted and roughly chopped
- 2 ready to eat figs, roughly chopped
- 2-3 drops vanilla extract
- ice cubes

Instructions
1. Place all ingredients except the ice in a blender and blend until smooth.
2. Three-quarters fill 3 tall glasses with ice and pour over the smoothie.
3. Optional – top each smoothie with a little grated or shaved dark chocolate.

PASSIONFRUIT VANILLA AND CHIA SEED SMOOTHIE

Nutrition: Cal 489; Fat 18 g; Carb 28 g; Protein 18 g
Serving 2; Cook time 10 min

Ingredients
- 1/3 cup Fresh 'n Fruity Vanilla Bean yoghurt

- 1/3 cup Anchor Blue milk
- 1/3 cup Chia seeds

Instructions
1. Soak chia in Anchor Blue milk overnight.
2. Combine soaked chia and milk with Fresh 'n Fruity Vanilla Bean yoghurt and blend.
3. Serve topped with fresh passionfuit and a chunky straw.

ALL-BERRY SMOOTHIE

Nutrition: Cal 365; Fat 5 g; Carb 28 g; Protein 11 g
Serving 1; Cook time 10 min

Ingredients
- 1 cup reduced fat milk
- 1/2 cup fruit like mixed berries
- 1–2 tsp honey (optional)
- 1 tbsp reduced fat natural yoghurt

Instructions
1. Pop all of the ingredients into a blender and blend until smooth. Serve in a tall glass.

HOT CHOCOLATE SMOOTHIE

Nutrition: Cal 443; Fat 3 g; Carb 63 g; Protein 10 g
Serving 1; Cook time 10 min

Ingredients
- 1 cup spinach
- 1 cup almond milk (unsweetened)
- ½ pear (peeled and cored)
- ¼ cup toasted hazelnuts
- 2 medjool dates
- 2 tablespoon cacao powder (to taste)
- ½ teaspoon vanilla extract
- whipped coconut cream (for topping)
- 1 tablespoon cacao nibs (optional)

Instructions
1. Blend spinach and almond milk until smooth.
2. Add the remaining ingredients, except coconut whipped cream. If using a high-speed blender, start blending again on low speed working up to high speed. Blend for 3-5 minutes, or until very hot. If using a regular blender, blend until smooth and heat gently on the stove or transfer to mugs and heat in a microwave.
3. Top with coconut whipped cream and cacao nibs.

APPLE PIE SMOOTHIE

Nutrition: Cal 321; Fat 4 g; Carb 73 g; Protein 4 g
Serving 1; Cook time 10 min

Ingredients
- ¼ cup hot water
- 2 tablespoon rolled oats
- 2 medjool dates (pitted)
- 1 cup spinach
- 1 cup almond milk
- 1 apple (cored and sliced)
- 1 teaspoon cinnamon (ground)
- 1/8 teaspoon nutmeg (ground)

Instructions
1. Add hot water, oats and dates to a blender. Let stand 5-10 minutes.
2. Add the remaining ingredients. Blend on low speed, increasing speed until very smooth. If using a high speed blender, continue blending using the soup function or high speed, until smoothie is hot.
3. Pour into a mug and sprinkle the top with extra cinnamon and nutmeg, if desired.

GINGERBREAD SPICE SMOOTHIE

Nutrition: Cal 223; Fat 10 g; Carb 30 g; Protein 5 g
Serving 1; Cook time 10 min

Ingredients
- 1 cup cauliflower (frozen)
- 1 tablespoon tahini
- 1 tablespoon molasses
- 1-3 teaspoon maple syrup
- ⅛ teaspoon ground nutmeg
- ⅛ teaspoon ground cloves
- 1 inch ginger root
- 1 cup cashew milk

Instructions
1. Blend cauliflower, tahini, molasses, maple syrup, nutmeg, cloves, ginger, and cashew milk until creamy and smoothie.

SKINNY MINT SMOOTHIE

Nutrition: Cal 378; Fat 12 g; Carb 74 g; Protein 5 g
Serving 1; Cook time 10 min

Ingredients
- 1 cups almond milk (unsweetened)
- ¾ cup spinach
- ¼ cup fresh mint
- 1 banana
- ¼ avocado
- 2 medjool dates
- 1 tablespoon cacao powder
- cacao nibs (optional)

Instructions
1. Blend spinach, mint, and almond milk until smooth.
2. Add remaining ingredients, and blend until smooth1 cups almond milk (unsweetened)

EPIC ALMOND SMOOTHIE

Nutrition: Cal 339; Fat 3 g; Carb 44 g; Protein 49g
Serving 1; Cook time 10 min

Ingredients
- 1 cup almond milk
- 2 tablespoon almonds
- 1 banana
- ½ teaspoon ground cinnamon
- 1 teaspoon maple syrup (or honey)
- ½ cup strawberries (frozen)

Instructions
1. Blend all ingredients until smooth. Pour into your favorite glass.

CHOCOLATE WEIGHT LOSS SMOOTHIE

Nutrition: Cal 406; Fat 29 g; Carb 30 g; Protein 4 g
Serving 1; Cook time 10 min

Ingredients
- 1 cup almond milk (unsweetened)
- 1 cup spinach
- ½ banana
- 2 tablespoon cacao powder
- 2 tablespoon almond butter
- 1 tablespoon hemp hearts
- 1 teaspoon ground cinnamon
- ⅛ teaspoon cayenne pepper

Instructions
1. Add leafy greens and liquid to blender, blending until all chunks are gone. Add in remaining ingredients and blend until smooth.

BERRY, CHIA, AND MINT SMOOTHIE

Nutrition: Cal 105; Fat 3 g; Carb 17 g; Protein 3 g
Serving 1; Cook time 10 min

Ingredients
- 1 c. sliced strawberries
- 1/2 c. raspberries
- 1/2 c. grated beet (from 1 medium beet)
- 1/3 c. mint leaves
- 1 tbsp. chia seeds
- 1 c. unsweetened almond milk

Instructions
1. Place berries, beet, mint, and chia seeds in resealable plastic bag or freezer-safe jar. Freeze overnight or longer.
2. When ready to prepare, add almond milk to blender, then add frozen ingredients. Blend until smooth. Serve in two tall glasses.

BERRY-ALMOND SMOOTHIE

Nutrition: Cal 360; Fat 19 g; Carb 45,6 g; Protein 4 g
Serving 1; Cook time 10 min

Ingredients
- ⅔ cup frozen raspberries
- ½ cup frozen sliced banana
- ½ cup plain unsweetened almond milk
- 5 tablespoons sliced almonds, divided
- ¼ teaspoon ground cinnamon
- ⅛ teaspoon ground cardamom
- ⅛ teaspoon vanilla extract
- ¼ cup blueberries
- 1 tablespoon unsweetened coconut flakes

Instructions
1. Blend raspberries, banana, almond milk, 3 tablespoons almonds, cinnamon, cardamom and vanilla in a blender until very smooth.
2. Pour the smoothie into a bowl and top with blueberries, the remaining 2 tablespoons almonds and coconut.

BANANA CREAM PIE SMOOTHIE

Nutrition: Cal 241; Fat 5 g; Carb 32 g; Protein 17 g
Serving 1; Cook time 10 min

Ingredients
- 1 ripe banana quartered
- 1/3 cup lowfat cottage cheese
- 1/3 cup lowfat milk
- 1 packet sweetner optional
- 1 tsp vanilla
- 1 cup ice
- Graham crackers

Instructions
1. Add all of your ingredients to a blender and blend until smooth.

TRIPLE BERRY SMOOTHIES

Nutrition: Cal 181; Fat 3 g; Carb 38 g; Protein 3 g
Serving 1; Cook time 10 min

Ingredients
- 2 cups strawberries
- 2/3 cup blueberries
- 2/3 cup blackberrie
- 1 cup packed baby kale
- 1/2 cup almond milk
- 2 tsps vanilla
- 2 tbls agave syrup (opt)

Instructions
1. Make the smoothie by adding berries and kale to blender. Process for 30 seconds or so to start to puree everything.
2. Add milk, vanilla, and agave syrup to blender. Process until smooth and then add a couple handfuls of ice and blend until smooth and somewhat thick.

PINEAPPLE COCONUT MANGO SMOOTHIE

Nutrition: Cal 134; Fat 3 g; Carb 31 g; Protein 4 g
Serving 1; Cook time 10 min

Ingredients
- 5.3 oz. vanilla yogurt
- 1/2 cup orange juice
- 1 cup fresh mango cubed
- 1 cup fresh pineapple cubed
- 1 tablespoon honey
- 1/4 cup coconut (I used roasted coconut from Trader Joe's)

Instructions
1. Combine all the ingredients in a blender and whip until smooth (you want the coconut to get fine and not stay chunky)

VERY BERRY SMOOTHIE

Nutrition: Cal 305; Fat 11 g; Carb 51 g; Protein 4 g
Serving 1; Cook time 10 min

Ingredients
- 1/2 of a ripe banana
- 1/2 cup blackberries
- 1/2cup raspberries

- 1/2 cup blueberries
- 5 oz. non-fat vanilla yogurt 1 cup ice

Instructions

1. Place all ingredients in blender and blend until smooth and ice is incorporated

EASY STRAWBERRY PINEAPPLE SMOOTHIE

Nutrition: Cal 224; Fat 1 g; Carb 55 g; Protein 4 g
Serving 1; Cook time 10 min

Ingredients

- 5.3 oz. vanilla non-fat yogurt
- 1 cup frozen pineapple chunks
- 1 cup frozen strawberries
- ⅓ cup orange juice

Instructions

1. Place all ingredients in blender and process until smooth.

PEACH & OATMEAL SMOOTHIE

Nutrition: Cal 626; Fat 3 g; Carb 34 g; Protein 24 g
Serving 1; Cook time 10 min

Ingredients

- 1/2 cup old-fashioned oats
- 1 1/2 cups frozen sliced peaches
- 1 cup Greek vanilla yogurt
- 1/2 cup milk
- 1-2 tbsp. honey
- 1/2 tsp. pure vanilla extract
- 1/2 tsp. ground cinnamon
- Additional peach slice, for garnish (optional)

Instructions

1. Place the oatmeal in a blender. Cover and process until the oatmeal resembles flour. Add the remaining ingredients. Cover and process until fully combined.
2. Pour the smoothie mixture into serving glasses. Garnish with peach slice, if desired.
3. Serve immediately.

KEY LIME PIE SMOOTHIE

Nutrition: Cal 254 Fat 3 g; Carb 55 g; Protein 17 g
Serving 1; Cook time 10 min

Ingredients

- 2 5.3-ounce containers key lime Greek yogurt
- 1/4 cup packed baby spinach
- 1 small banana
- 1/2 cup pineapple chunks
- 1 cup almond milk
- tablespoons key lime juice
- 1 lime wedge
- 1-2 cups ice
- 1/2 cup crushed graham crackers for garnish
- Whipped cream for garnish

Instructions

1. Add all ingredients through lime juice to a blender, pulse to puree.
2. Add ice to reach desired consistency. Pulse to blend.
3. Place graham cracker crumbs on a small plate.
4. Run lime wedge around edge of 2 glasses. Dip edges in graham cracker crumbs.
5. Pour smoothie into glasses. Garnish with whipped cream and sprinkle with more graham cracker crumbs

FRUITY POWER SMOOTHIE

Nutrition: Cal 166; Fat 3 g; Carb 40 g; Protein 4 g
Serving 1; Cook time 10 min

Ingredients

- 2 oz Pomegranate Juice
- 3 oz Orange Juice
- 1/2 up sliced banana
- 1/2 cup frozen mixed berries
- 1/4 cup non-fat vanilla yogurt
- 2 tablespoons dry milk
- 1 tablespoon honey

Instructions

1. Add all ingredients in a blender and process until smooth

MANGO RASPBERRY SUNSHINE YOGURT SMOOTHIE

Nutrition: Cal 148; Fat 3 g; Carb 34 g; Protein 4 g
Serving 1; Cook time 10 min

Ingredients

- 2/3 cup frozen mango chunks
- 1/2 cup orange juice
- 1/4 cup vanilla yogurt
- 2 tablespoons water
- 1 cup frozen raspberries
- 1/2 cup orange juice
- 1 tablespoon honey
- 1/4 cup vanilla yogurt
- 1 tablespoon water

Instructions

1. Str In a blender combine the mango chunks, ½ cup orange juice, ¼ cup vanilla yogurt and 2 tablespoons water.
2. Mix well and divide between 3 8 oz glasses
3. Clean out blender then combine the raspberries, ½ cup orange juice, honey, ¼ cup yogurt and 1 tablespoon water

AWBERRY MANGO PEACH SMOOTHIE

Nutrition: Cal 215; Fat 3 g; Carb 53 g; Protein 2 g
Serving 1; Cook time 10 min

Ingredients

- 1/2 cup frozen, peeled mango chunks, partially thawed
- 1/2 cups frozen strawberries
- 1 cup fresh peach slices (2 medium peaches, pitted)
- 1 well ripened banana
- 2 cups chilled pineapple juice

Instructions

1. Add all ingredients to a blender and process until smooth. Serve immediately.

TROPICAL SMOOTHIE

Nutrition: Cal 226; Fat 3 g; Carb 56 g; Protein 3 g
Serving 1; Cook time 10 min

Ingredients
- 2 cups (10 oz) frozen cubed pineapple*
- 1 cup (5 oz) frozen cubed mangoes
- 1 medium ripe banana, peeled
- 2 medium (5 oz total) mandarin oranges or clementines, peeled
- 1 cup coconut water,** chilled
- 1/2 tsp coconut extract

Instructions
1. Add all ingredients to a blender and process until smooth. Serve immediately.

WILD BLUEBERRY POMEGRANATE SMOOTHIE

Nutrition: Cal 243; Fat 3 g; Carb 53 g; Protein 1 g
Serving 1; Cook time 10 min

Ingredients
- 1/2 cups frozen wild blueberries
- cup pomegranate juice
- 2/3 cup plain Greek yogurt
- 1/2 cup water
- large ripe banana (peeled and frozen if desired)
- Honey to taste, as needed

Instructions
1. Add all ingredients to a blender and process until smooth. Serve immediately.

BANANA ALMOND FLAX SMOOTHIE

Nutrition: Cal 392; Fat 3 g; Carb 43 g; Protein 11 g
Serving 1; Cook time 10 min

Ingredients
- 1 medium well ripened banana, peeled diced into pieces, frozen
- 2/3 cup unsweetened almond milk
- 1/3 cup fat free plain Greek yogurt
- 1 1/2 Tbsp creamy almond butter
- 1 Tbsp ground flaxseed meal
- 1 tsp honey
- 3 /4 drops almond extract
- 4 ice cubes (optional)

Instructions
1. Add all ingredients to a blender and process until smooth. Serve immediately.

CINNAMON BUN BREAKFAST SMOOTHIE

Nutrition: Cal 213; Fat 5 g; Carb 32 g; Protein 4 g
Serving 1; Cook time 10 min

Ingredients
- 1/2 frozen ripe banana
- 1/2 cup almond milk (original)
- 1/2 cup cold water
- 1/4 tsp vanilla extract
- 1/4 tsp ground cinnamon , plus more to taste
- 1/4 cup quick oats
- 3 oz low fat Greek yogurt or 1 oz low fat cream cheese
- 3 4 ice cubes

Instructions
1. Add all ingredients to a blender and process until smooth. Serve immediately.

STRAWBERRY COCONUT OAT SMOOTHIE

Nutrition: Cal 260; Fat 3 g; Carb 45 g; Protein 11 g
Serving 1; Cook time 10 min

Ingredients
- 3/4 cup frozen diced strawberries
- 1/2 (5.3 oz) container Coconut Greek Yogurt (I used Chobani 2%)
- 1/2 cup almond milk coconut milk blend
- 1/2 cup water
- 1/4 cup quick oats
- 1/2 large , peeled and frozen very ripe banana

Instructions
1. Combine all ingredients in a blender and process until well pureed. Add a few tablespoons more of the almond milk coconut milk blend or water to thin as desired

PEACH & OAT BREAKFAST SMOOTHIE

Nutrition: Cal 252; Fat 3 g; Carb 48 g; Protein 8 g
Serving 1; Cook time 10 min

Ingredients
- 1/2 cups frozen peach chunks
- 1 cup almond coconut milk blend or original almond milk
- 1 (5.3 oz) container greek yogurt, mango, peach, strawberry or coconut flavor
- 1 very ripe banana , peeled and frozen
- 1/2 cup oats (old fashioned or quick, either are fine)
- 1/2 cup cold water

Instructions
1. Add all ingredients to a blender and process until smooth. Serve immediately.

CABBAGE AND BERRY PURPLE SMOOTHIE

Nutrition: Cal 142; Fat 3 g; Carb 28 g; Protein 4 g
Serving 1; Cook time 10 min

Ingredients
- 8 oz. purple cabbage (half of a small head)
- 1 cup frozen blueberries
- 1 cup frozen strawberries
- 1 ripe banana , peeled and frozen
- 1 (5.3 oz) container cherry Greek yogurt (or strawberry)
- 1 cup chilled Hibiscus tea*
- 1/2 cup almond milk

Instructions
1. Add all ingredients to a blender and process until smooth. Serve immediately.

STRAWBERRY BANANA OAT SMOOTHIE

Nutrition: Cal 275; Fat 3 g; Carb 54 g; Protein 4 g
Serving 1; Cook time 10 min

Ingredients
- 1 cup unsweetened almond milk or 1% milk
- 1/2 cup fat free plain Greek yogurt
- 2 cups (9 oz) frozen strawberries
- 1 1/2 ripe medium bananas
- 1/2 cup quick oats or old fashioned oats
- 1 Tbsp honey
- 1/2 tsp vanilla extract

Instructions
1. Add all ingredients to a blender, cover and blend until smooth. Serve immediately.

CRANBERRY POMEGRANATE SMOOTHIE

Nutrition: Cal 178; Fat 1 g; Carb 38 g; Protein 4 g
Serving 1; Cook time 10 min

Ingredients
- 1 cup cranberries, frozen
- 1/2 cup pomegranate juice
- 1/2 cup original almond milk
- 1 (5.3 oz) container vanilla greek yogurt
- 1 very ripe banana, peeled
- 1 cup ice

Instructions
1. Add all ingredients to blender and blend until smooth. Serve immediately.

PUMPKIN CHEESECAKE BREAKFAST SMOOTHIE

Nutrition: Cal 371; Fat 16 g; Carb 55 g; Protein 4 g
Serving 1; Cook time 10 min

Ingredients
- 1 cup almond milk (preferably original)
- 1/2 cup pumpkin puree, cold
- 1 small frozen well ripened banana*
- 1/4 cup quick oats
- 1 oz cream cheese, regular or low-fat
- 1/4 tsp ground cinnamon
- 1 pinch ground nutmeg
- 1 pinch ground ginger
- 1 Tbsp crushed graham crackers or graham pie crust (optional)

Instructions
1. Add all ingredients to a blender (except graham crackers if using). Cover and blend until well pureed then serve topped with crushed graham crackers if desired.

BANANA BERRY SMOOTHIES

Nutrition: Cal 302; Fat 3 g; Carb 68 g; Protein 4 g
Serving 1; Cook time 10 min

Ingredients
- 2 ripe bananas
- 1 1/2 cups frozen blueberries
- 1 1/4 cups raspberry sherbet
- 3/4 cup fat free frozen yogurt
- 1 cup berry blend juice, plus 1/4 cup more as needed
- 8 ice cubes

Instructions
1. Add bananas, blueberries, raspberry sherbet, frozen yogurt and berry blend juice to a blender, cover with lid and blend until well blended.
2. Add ice and blend until ice is fully processed and ice pieces no longer remain.

RASPBERRY BANANA SMOOTHIES

Nutrition: Cal 288; Fat 2 g; Carb 53 g; Protein 4 g
Serving 1; Cook time 10 min

Ingredients
- 1/2 cup fresh raspberries (frozen would be fine too)
- 1 ripe banana, peeled and frozen
- 1/2 cup original almond milk
- 1 (5.3 oz) container strawberry or raspberry Greek yogurt
- 1/4 cup water
- 3 - 4 ice cubes (optional)

Instructions
1. Add all ingredients to a blender and puree until smooth.

PINA COLADA OAT BREAKFAST SMOOTHIES

Nutrition: Cal 241; Fat 4 g; Carb 47 g; Protein 4 g
Serving 1; Cook time 10 min

Ingredients
- 2 cups diced pineapple (preferably fresh), chilled
- 1 1/2 cups coconut almond milk blend
- 1 cup cold water
- 1 (5.3 oz) container greek yogurt, such as Chobani
- 3/4 cup rolled oats (old fashioned or quick)
- 1 large very ripe banana peeled and frozen

Instructions
1. Add all ingredients to a blender and process until smooth.

PAPAYA MANGO SMOOTHIE WITH LEMON AND GINGER

Nutrition: Cal 167; Fat 3 g; Carb 33 g; Protein 4 g
Serving 1; Cook time 10 min

Ingredients
- 1/2 cups unsweetened almond milk
- 2 cups roughly chopped papaya
- 1 tablespoon freshly squeezed lemon juice
- 2 teaspoons minced fresh ginger
- 1/8 teaspoon ground cinnamon
- 1/8 teaspoon finely grated lemon zest
- 1 tablespoon maple syrup, or more to taste
- 1/4 cup frozen mango cubes
- 1 cup ice cubes
- 1 teaspoon hulled hemp seeds, for topping (optional)

Instructions
1. Blend all ingredients (except hemp seeds, if using) together in a blender until smooth. Sprinkle with hemp seeds and serve.

PAPAYA BANANA SMOOTHIE WITH PEANUT BUTTER

Nutrition: Cal 293; Fat 13 g; Carb 42 g; Protein 4 g
Serving 1; Cook time 10 min

Ingredients
- 2 cups chopped fresh papaya
- half a lime, zested and juiced
- 1 frozen banana
- 1 cup almond milk
- 1 teaspoon maple syrup
- 1 tablespoon peanut butter
- 1/2 cup ice
- chia seeds for topping
- hulled hemp seeds, for topping

Instructions
1. Combine all the ingredients (except chia and hemp seeds, if using) together in a blender and blend until smooth. Sprinkle with seeds of your choice and serve.

GUAVA SMOOTHIE WITH STRAWBERRIES AND BANANA

Nutrition: Cal 199; Fat 3 g; Carb 39 g; Protein 4 g
Serving 1; Cook time 10 min

Ingredients
- 1/2 cup almond milk
- 3 guavas, seeds removed
- 1 frozen sliced banana
- 1 cup chopped strawberries
- 1 tablespoon maple syrup
- hulled hemp seeds, for topping (optional)

Instructions
1. Combine all the ingredients (except hemp seeds) together in a blender and blend until smooth.

CREAMY DRAGON FRUIT SMOOTHIE

Nutrition: Cal 251; Fat 10 g; Carb 37 g; Protein 4 g
Serving 1; Cook time 10 min

Ingredients
- 1 dragon fruit fresh or frozen
- 2 bananas frozen
- 1/2 cup mixed berries frozen
- 2 tablespoons quick oats
- 3 tablespoons coconut milk
- 1 tablespoon almond butter

Instructions
1. Place all of the ingredients in your blender, and blend until you get a creamy smoothie.

BLUEBERRY PAPAYA SMOOTHIE

Nutrition: Cal 235; Fat 3 g; Carb 42 g; Protein 5 g
Serving 1; Cook time 10 min

Ingredients
- 1 cup fresh papaya, peeled, deseeded and cubed
- 1/2 cup frozen wild blueberries
- 1 banana, divided
- 1/2 cup almond milk
- 1/2 teaspoons chia seeds, divided
- 2 teaspoons date syrup
- 1 cup ice
- almond granola for garnish
- flaked coconut for garnish

Instructions
1. Place all of the ingredients in your blender, and blend until you get a creamy smoothie.

TANGY BAOBAB SUNSHINE SMOOTHIE

Nutrition: Cal 247; Fat 4 g; Carb 37 g; Protein 4 g
Serving 1; Cook time 10 min

Ingredients
- the water and meat from 1 Thai coconut (or 1 ½ cup water)
- 1 banana, frozen
- 1 cup pineapple, frozen
- 1 cup mango, frozen
- 1 passion fruit
- 1 tsp baobab powder
- 1/2 tsp camu camu powder (optional)
- pinch turmeric powder (optional)

Instructions
1. Place all of the ingredients in your blender, and blend until you get a creamy smoothie.

SUPERFOOD BLUEBERRY SPINACH SMOOTHIE

Nutrition: Cal 218; Fat 3 g; Carb 45 g; Protein 4 g
Serving 1; Cook time 10 min

Ingredients
- 1 large ripe banana
- 1 cup spinach leafs
- 2/3 cup frozen wild blueberries
- 1/3 cup unsweetened almond milk
- 1 teaspoon hemp seeds
- 1/2 teaspoon flax meal/seeds
- 1/4 teaspoon moringa powder

Instructions
1. Place all of the ingredients in your blender, and blend until you get a creamy smoothie.

RASPBERRY PEACH SMOOTHIE

Nutrition: Cal 376; Fat 3 g; Carb 57 g; Protein 4 g
Serving 1; Cook time 10 min

Ingredients
- 1/2 cup frozen peach slices
- 1/2 cup frozen raspberries
- 1/2 cup vanilla Greek yogurt or dairy free yogurt
- 1/4 cup almond milk
- Sweetener to taste (optional)
- 1/4 cup fresh raspberries
- 1 tablespoon diced fresh peaches
- 1 tablespoon granola

Instructions
1. Place all of the ingredients in your blender, and blend until you get a creamy smoothie.

PEACH COBBLER SMOOTHIE

Nutrition: Cal 367; Fat 4 g; Carb 59 g; Protein 4 g
Serving 1; Cook time 10 min

Ingredients
- 2 small peaches or 1 large peach (or 1 cup frozen peaches)
- 1 cup of ice
- 1/2 cup of almond milk
- 1/3 cup of vanilla Greek yogurt (or almond milk yogurt)
- 1/4 cup oats, uncooked
- Stevia or sweetener to taste (I used about 3 drops of stevia)
- 1/4 cup of granola, for topping

Instructions
1. Place all of the ingredients in your blender, and blend until you get a creamy smoothie.

APPLE CIDER VINEGAR

Nutrition: Cal 112; Fat 4 g; Carb 24 g; Protein 4 g
Serving 1; Cook time 10 min

Ingredients
- 1 frozen banana
- 1/2 cup orange juice
- 1 tablespoon apple cider vinegar
- 1 cup ice
- 1/2 cup vanilla yogurt
- 1/2 teaspoon grated ginger

Instructions
1. Place all of the ingredients in your blender, and blend until you get a creamy smoothie.

FRUIT & YOGURT SMOOTHIE

Nutrition: Cal 279; Fat 3 g; Carb 56 g; Protein 4 g
Serving 1; Cook time 10 min

Ingredients
- 2 servings 10 mins
- 3/4 cup nonfat plain yogurt
- 1/2 cup 100% pure fruit juice
- 1 1/2 cups (6 1/2 ounces) frozen fruit

Instructions
1. Puree yogurt with juice in a blender until smooth. With the motor running, add fruit through the hole in the lid and continue to puree until smooth.

UNICORN SMOOTHIE

Nutrition: Cal 257; Fat 3 g; Carb 52 g; Protein 4 g
Serving 1; Cook time 10 min

Ingredients
- 1/2 cups low-fat milk, divided
- 1/2 cups low-fat vanilla yogurt, divided
- 3 large bananas, divided
- 1cup frozen blackberries or blueberries
- 1cup frozen mango chunks
- cup frozen raspberries or strawberries

Instructions
1. Place all of the ingredients in your blender, and blend until you get a creamy smoothie.

PERFECT BERRY SMOOTHIE

Nutrition: Cal 297; Fat 3 g; Carb 28 g; Protein 13 g
Serving 1; Cook time 10 min

Ingredients
- 2 cups frozen mixed berries
- 1 banana (room temperature)
- 1/2 cup Greek yogurt*
- 1/4 cup milk (or almond milk or oat milk)
- 1/2 tablespoons maple syrup, honey, or agave syrup
- 1/2 cup ice
- Optional add-ins: 1 tablespoon almond butter, ¼ teaspoon vanilla, fresh mint leaves or basil leaves

Instructions
1. Place all of the ingredients in your blender, and blend until you get a creamy smoothie.

PERFECT STRAWBERRY SMOOTHIE

Nutrition: Cal 245; Fat 4 g; Carb 51 g; Protein 4 g
Serving 2; Cook time 10 min

Ingredients
- 2 cups frozen strawberries
- 1 banana (room temperature)
- ¼ cup Greek yogurt*
- 1 cup milk (or almond milk or oat milk)
- 1 ½ tablespoons maple syrup, honey, or agave syrup
- ½ cup ice

Instructions
1. Place all of the ingredients in your blender, and blend until you get a creamy smoothie.

CHIA SEED SMOOTHIE

Nutrition: Cal 304; Fat 3 g; Carb 48 g; Protein 4 g
Serving 1; Cook time 10 min

Ingredients
- 2 cups frozen strawberries (or any frozen berry)
- 1 banana (room temperature)
- ½ cup Greek yogurt*
- ¾ cup milk (or almond milk or oat milk)
- 2 tablespoons chia seeds
- 1 ½ tablespoons maple syrup, honey, or agave syrup
- ½ cup ice

Instructions
1. Place all of the ingredients in your blender, and blend until you get a creamy smoothie.

PERFECT BANANA SMOOTHIE

Nutrition: Cal 171; Fat 3 g; Carb 232g; Protein 7 g
Serving 1; Cook time 10 min

Ingredients
- 2 medium ripe bananas (room temperature)
- 1 ½ cups ice
- 1/4 cup Greek yogurt*
- 1/2 to 3/4 cup milk or nondairy milk

Instructions

1. Place all of the ingredients in your blender, and blend until you get a creamy smoothie.

CHOCOLATE BLACK BEAN SMOOTHIE

Nutrition: Cal 452; Fat 3 g; Carb 77 g; Protein 4 g
Serving 1; Cook time 10 min

Ingredients
- 1 frozen banana
- 1 cup frozen cauliflower
- 1/2 cup black beans
- 1-2 medjool dates pitted
- 1 cup oat milk or milk of choice
- 1 tablespoon hemp seeds
- 1 tablespoon cocoa powder
- 1 teaspoon ground cinnamon

Instructions
1. Place all of the ingredients in your blender, and blend until you get a creamy smoothie.

AMAZING APPLE CINNAMON WEIGHT GAIN SMOOTHIE

Nutrition: Cal 775; Fat 11 g; Carb 86 g; Protein 4 g
Serving 1; Cook time 10 min

Ingredients
- 1 apple
- ½ banana
- 2 tablespoons peanut butter
- 3 tablespoons hemp seeds
- ½ cup oats rolled, old fashioned
- 1 cup oat milk any milk can be substituted

Instructions
1. Place all of the ingredients in your blender, and blend until you get a creamy smoothie.

MATCHA KIWI NICE SMOOTHIE

Nutrition: Cal 7001; Fat 3 g; Carb 86 g; Protein 4 g
Serving 1; Cook time 10 min

Ingredients
- 3 frozen bananas
- 2 frozen kiwi
- 2 dates, pitted
- 1 tsp matcha powder
- 1/2 cup plant milk (like almond, oat, or flax milk)

Instructions
1. Place all of the ingredients in your blender, and blend until you get a creamy smoothie.

PINK MERMAID SMOOTHIE

Nutrition: Cal 268; Fat 3 g; Carb 71 g; Protein 4 g
Serving 1; Cook time 10 min

Ingredients
- splash milk of choice
- 2 cups frozen pineapple
- 1 frozen banana
- 1 ½ teaspoon black goji berry powder

Instructions

1. Place all of the ingredients in your blender, and blend until you get a creamy smoothie.

COTTON CANDY SMOOTHIE

Nutrition: Cal 269; Fat 3 g; Carb 52 g; Protein 4 g
Serving 1; Cook time 10 min

Ingredients
- 1 cup frozen strawberries
- 1 cup frozen pineapple
- ½ frozen banana

Instructions
1. Place all of the ingredients in your blender, and blend until you get a creamy smoothie.

PURPLE SMOOTHIE

Nutrition: Cal 296; Fat 3 g; Carb 50 g; Protein 4 g
Serving 1; Cook time 10 min

Ingredients
- 1 frozen banana
- 1 teaspoon butterfly pea powder

Instructions
1. Place all of the ingredients in your blender, and blend until you get a creamy smoothie.

BERRY GINGER SMOOTHIE

Nutrition: Cal 136; Fat 3 g; Carb 30 g; Protein 3 g
Serving 1; Cook time 10 min

Ingredients
- 3/4 cup frozen strawberries
- 3/4 cup frozen raspberries
- 1/2 banana, peeled
- 1 large orange, peeled
- 1 inch chunk ginger, peeled
- 1 cup 240 ml almond milk

Instructions
1. Place all of the ingredients in your blender, and blend until you get a creamy smoothie.

SALTED CARAMEL SMOOTHIE

Nutrition: Cal 446; Fat 32 g; Carb 39 g; Protein 4 g
Serving 1; Cook time 10 min

Ingredients
- 1/4 cup milk dairy or plant based
- 2 tablespoons cream cheese or yoghurt
- 1 banana frozen if possible
- 3 dates
- 1/4 teaspoon salt fine sea salt or himalayan pink salt

Instructions
1. Place all of the ingredients in your blender, and blend until you get a creamy smoothie.

BERRY KIWI YOGURT SMOOTHIE

Nutrition: Cal 661; Fat 3 g; Carb 127 g; Protein 14 g
Serving 1; Cook time 10 min

Ingredients
- 2 fruit (2" dia) Kiwi fruit

- 2 medium Banana
- 1 cup Whole milk
- 1/2 container (8 oz) Plain yogurt
- 1 cup Raspberries
- 1 cup Blueberries

Instructions
1. Place all of the ingredients in your blender, and blend until you get a creamy smoothie.

APPLE BERRY YOGURT SMOOTHIE

Nutrition: Cal 415; Fat 3 g; Carb 95 g; Protein 4 g
Serving 1; Cook time 10 min

Ingredients
- 1/2 cup Apple juice
- 1/2 cup (8 fl oz) Vanilla yogurt
- 1/4 cup Blueberries
- 1/4 cup, unthawed Blackberries, frozen
- 1/4 cup, unthawed Raspberries
- 1/2 tbsp Raw Agave Nectar

Instructions
1. Place all of the ingredients in your blender, and blend until you get a creamy smoothie.

PEANUT BUTTER BANANA OATMEAL SMOOTHIE

Nutrition: Cal 293; Fat 3 g; Carb 41 g; Protein 4 g
Serving 1; Cook time 10 min

Ingredients
- 2 ripe bananas
- 1 cup low fat milk (any kind woks)
- 1 cup non-fat vanilla Greek yogurt
- 1 cup oats (old fashioned)
- ¼ cup natural peanut butter
- 1 teaspoon cinnamon
- 2-3 large scoops ice (or more to taste)

Instructions
1. Place all of the ingredients in your blender, and blend until you get a creamy smoothie.

MANGO PEACH AND STRAWBERRY SMOOTHIE

Nutrition: Cal 215; Fat 3 g; Carb 53 g; Protein 4 g
Serving 1; Cook time 10 min

Ingredients
- 1 1/2 cup frozen, peeled mango chunks, partially thawed
- 1 1/2 cups frozen strawberries
- 1 cup fresh peach slices (2 medium peaches, pitted)
- 1 well ripened banana
- 2 cups chilled pineapple juice

Instructions
1. Place all of the ingredients in your blender, and blend until you get a creamy smoothie.

BERRY BANANA BREAKFAST SMOOTHIE

Nutrition: Cal 332; Fat 3 g; Carb 77 g; Protein 4 g
Serving 1; Cook time 10 min

Ingredients
- 1 banana

- ½ cup strawberries
- ½ cup blueberries
- ½ cup raspberries
- 1 apple cored and sliced
- 1 cup almond milk

Instructions
1. Place all of the ingredients in your blender, and blend until you get a creamy smoothie.

SKINNY ORANGE DREAM BREAKFAST SMOOTHIE

Nutrition: Cal 129; Fat 0 g; Carb 25 g; Protein 4 g
Serving 1; Cook time 10 min

Ingredients
- 1 orange peeled
- 1 teaspoon vanilla extract
- 1 teaspoon honey
- 1/4 cup Almond milk
- 1/4 cup Greek yogurt
- 1/2 cup ice

Instructions
1. Place all of the ingredients in your blender, and blend until you get a creamy smoothie.

CHOCOLATE, BANANA AND ALMOND BUTTER BREAKFAST SMOOTHIES

Nutrition: Cal 151; Fat 3 g; Carb 24 g; Protein 4 g
Serving 1; Cook time 10 min

Ingredients
- cup unsweetened almond milk
- 1 frozen banana
- 1 tablespoon homemade fat free chocolate syrup
- 1 tablespoon almond butter
- 1 large handful ice

Instructions
1. Place all of the ingredients in your blender, and blend until you get a creamy smoothie.

BANANA OATMEAL BREAKFAST SMOOTHIE

Nutrition: Cal 279; Fat 3 g; Carb 46 g; Protein 4 g
Serving 1; Cook time 10 min

Ingredients
- 1/4 cup old-fashioned rolled oats
- 1/2 cup plain low-fat yogurt
- banana cut into thirds
- 1/2 cup almond milk
- 1 teaspoon honey optional
- 1/4 teaspoon ground cinnamon

Instructions
1. Place all of the ingredients in your blender, and blend until you get a creamy smoothie.

STRAWBERRY BANANA BREAKFAST SMOOTHIE

Nutrition: Cal 165; Fat 3 g; Carb 37 g; Protein 4 g
Serving 1; Cook time 10 min

Ingredients
- 1/2 cup strawberries

- 1 banana
- 1 cup raw spinach
- 1/2 cup almond milk
- 1 teaspoon vanilla extract

Instructions
1. Place all of the ingredients in your blender, and blend until you get a creamy smoothie.

CHOCOLATE BANANA BREAKFAST SMOOTHIE

Nutrition: Cal 368; Fat 3 g; Carb 46 g; Protein 4 g
Serving 1; Cook time 10 min

Ingredients
- 1 banana
- 10 almonds
- 1 cup Almond milk
- 1 cup Greek yogurt I like unsweetened, but vanilla flavor is excellent here1 tablespoon cocoa powder

Instructions
1. Place all of the ingredients in your blender, and blend until you get a creamy smoothie.

BERRY GREEN BREAKFAST SMOOTHIE

Nutrition: Cal 95; Fat 3 g; Carb 22 g; Protein 4 g
Serving 1; Cook time 10 min

Ingredients
- 1/2 cup strawberries
- 1/2 cup blueberries
- 1/4 cup raspberries
- 2 cups spinach
- 1 cup water
- 1 cup ice

Instructions
1. Place all of the ingredients in your blender, and blend until you get a creamy smoothie.

STRAWBERRY BLUEBERRY CHIA SMOOTHIE

Nutrition: Cal 216; Fat 3 g; Carb 239g; Protein 4 g
Serving 1; Cook time 10 min

Ingredients
- 1 cup unsweetened almond milk (or your choice of milk)
- 1 cup fresh strawberries, washed, hulled, and halved
- 1/2 cup frozen blueberries
- 2 teaspoons honey (vegans can use maple syrup)
- 2 teaspoons chia seeds

Instructions
1. Place all of the ingredients in your blender, and blend until you get a creamy smoothie.

GINGERBREAD SMOOTHIE

Nutrition: Cal 231; Fat 3 g; Carb 42 g; Protein 4 g
Serving 1; Cook time 10 min

Ingredients
- 1/2 cups unsweetened plant milk
- 2 frozen bananas, broken into chunks
- 2 tablespoons chia seeds
- 1 tablespoon blackstrap molasses
- 1/4 teaspoon ground cinnamon
- 1/2 teaspoon ground ginger
- 1/8 teaspoon allspice

Instructions
1. Place all of the ingredients in your blender, and blend until you get a creamy smoothie.

PEACH WITH OAT SMOOTHIE

Nutrition: Cal 142; Fat 3 g; Carb 28 g; Protein 4 g
Serving 1; Cook time 10 min

Ingredients
- 2 ripe peaches (quartered, pits removed*)
- 1 Tbsp chia seeds
- 1/4 cup rolled oats (gluten-free for GF eaters)
- 1/2 frozen banana (peeled before freezing)
- 1/4 cup fresh orange juice
- 1/2 cup unsweetened almond milk
- 1 Tbsp agave, maple syrup, or a pinch of stevia (*optional /for added sweetness / or honey for non-vegan*

Instructions
1. Place all of the ingredients in your blender, and blend until you get a creamy smoothie.

MATCHA SMOOTHIE

Nutrition: Cal 210; Fat 3 g; Carb 28 g; Protein 4 g
Serving 1; Cook time 10 min

Ingredients
- tsp matcha powder
- 1/2 cup plant milk (like almond, oat, or flax milk)

Instructions
1. Place all of the ingredients in your blender, and blend until you get a creamy smoothie.

PEACH SMOOTHIE

Nutrition: Cal 142; Fat 3 g; Carb 28 g; Protein 4 g
Serving 1; Cook time 10 min

Ingredients
- 2 ripe peaches (quartered, pits removed*)
- 1 Tbsp chia seeds
- 1/2 frozen banana (peeled before freezing)
- 1/2 cup unsweetened almond milk

Instructions
1. Place all of the ingredients in your blender, and blend until you get a creamy smoothie.

CARAMEL SMOOTHIE

Nutrition: Cal 443; Fat 32 g; Carb 35 g; Protein 4 g
Serving 1; Cook time 10 min

Ingredients
- 1/4 cup milk dairy or plant based
- teaspoon caramel

Instructions
1. Place all of the ingredients in your blender, and blend until you get a creamy smoothie.

ALMOND BUTTER SMOOTHIES

Nutrition: Cal 154; Fat 2 g; Carb 25g; Protein 3 g
Serving 1; Cook time 10 min

Ingredients
- 1 tablespoon almond butter
- 1 cup unsweetened almond milk
- 1 large handful ice

Instructions
1. Place all of the ingredients in your blender, and blend until you get a creamy smoothie.

DETOX SMOOTHIES

CREAMY KALE SMOOTHIE

Nutrition: Cal 296; Fat 39 g; Carb 45 g; Protein 4 g
Serving 1; Cook time 10 min

Ingredients
- 1 cup coarsely chopped kale
- 1/2 cup frozen pineapple chunks
- 1/2 cup plain Greek yogurt
- 1/2 cup unsweetened almond milk
- 1 tsp honey

Instructions
1. Place all of the ingredients in your blender, and blend until you get a creamy smoothie.

ANTIOXIDANT BERRY AVOCADO SMOOTHIE

Nutrition: Cal 305; Fat 3 g; Carb 42 g; Protein 4 g
Serving 1; Cook time 10 min

Ingredients
- 1 cup Sprouts Sliced Frozen Avocados
- 1 cup Sprouts Whole Antioxidant Blend
- 1 banana
- 1 handful spinach leaves
- 2 tablespoons ground flax seeds
- 1 and ¼ cups unsweetened almond milk

Instructions
1. Place all of the ingredients in your blender, and blend until you get a creamy smoothie.

APPLE SMOOTHIE

Nutrition: Cal 376; Fat 3 g; Carb 49 g; Protein 9 g
Serving 1; Cook time 10 min

Ingredients
- 1/2 cups baby kale
- 1 large apple, cored and roughly chopped
- 2 tablespoons cashew butter or other nut butter
- 2 teaspoons honey
- 5-6 ice cubes
- 1 cup unsweetened almond milk or other milk

Instructions
1. Place all of the ingredients in your blender, and blend until you get a creamy smoothie.

GREEN SMOOTHIE

Nutrition: Cal 272; Fat 3 g; Carb 62 g; Protein 4 g
Serving 1; Cook time 10 min

Ingredients
- 1 cup cold water
- 1 full romaine heart
- 1-2 ounces baby spinach
- 1 frozen banana, chopped
- 1/2 Pink Lady or Fuji apple
- 1/2 lemon, peel removed
- 1 knob fresh ginger (about 1 inch)
- 4-5 leaves fresh min
- 1 teaspoon chia seeds

Instructions
1. Place all of the ingredients in your blender, and blend until you get a creamy smoothie.

BERRY SMOOTHIE

Nutrition: Cal 396; Fat 3 g; Carb 69 g; Protein 12 g
Serving 1; Cook time 10 min

Ingredients
- 2 leaves kale, rinsed, ribs removed and torn
- 1/3 cup fresh blackberries
- 1/3 cup fresh blueberries
- 1/3 cup fresh raspberries
- 1 tablespoon chia seeds
- 1 tablespoon chopped walnuts
- 1 tablespoon freshly squeezed lemon juice
- 1 teaspoon grated fresh ginger
- 1 cup frozen strawberries
- 3/4 cup tart cherry juice
- fresh fruit, for garnish (optional)

Instructions
1. Place all of the ingredients in your blender, and blend until you get a creamy smoothie.

LIVER SMOOTHIE

Nutrition: Cal 189; Fat 3 g; Carb 48 g; Protein 4 g
Serving 1; Cook time 10 min

Ingredients
- 1 ripe banana, peeled
- 1/2 green apple, cored and chopped
- 1 medium-sized carrot, peeled and chopped
- 1 handful baby spinach
- 1 (1/4-inch) nub turmeric root, peeled
- 1 Tbsp fresh parsley, chopped
- 3 walnut halves
- 2 Tbsp Hemp Protein Powder
- 1/2 lemon, juiced
- 1 pinch cinnamon, optional

Instructions
1. Place all of the ingredients in your blender, and blend until you get a creamy smoothie.

5-INGREDIENT SMOOTHIE

Nutrition: Cal 181; Fat 3 g; Carb 41 g; Protein 4 g
Serving 1; Cook time 10 min

Ingredients
- 1 cup frozen berries
- 1 cup organic spinach or kale
- 1/2 cup bananas (previously peeled, sliced & frozen)
- 1 Tbsp flaxseed meal
- 1 cup fruit juice (I mixed pomegranate & orange = my faves)
- 2 Tbsp silken tofu (*optional*)

Instructions
1. Place all of the ingredients in your blender, and blend until you get a creamy smoothie.

PINEAPPLE-GRAPEFRUIT SMOOTHIE

Nutrition: Cal 102; Fat 0,2 g; Carb 25 g; Protein 4 g
Serving 1; Cook time 10 min

Ingredients
- 1 cup plain coconut water
- 1 cup frozen diced pineapple
- 1 cup packed baby spinach
- 1 small grapefruit, peeled and segmented, plus any juice squeezed from the membranes
- ½ teaspoon grated fresh ginger
- 1 cup ice

Instructions
1. Place all of the ingredients in your blender, and blend until you get a creamy smoothie.

VITAMIX TRIPLE BERRY SMOOTHIE

Nutrition: Cal 275; Fat 3 g; Carb 60 g; Protein 4 g
Serving 1; Cook time 10 min

Ingredients
- 1/2 cup blueberries, frozen
- 1/2 cup raspberries, frozen
- 1/2 cup red grapes
- 1/2 cup strawberries, frozen
- 1/2 cup vanilla nonfat frozen yogurt
- 1/2 cup water
- 1 cup ice
- 1 scoop

Instructions
1. Place all of the ingredients in your blender, and blend until you get a creamy smoothie.

APPLE PIE SMOOTHIE

Nutrition: Cal 212; Fat 3 g; Carb 130 g; Protein 4 g
Serving 1; Cook time 10 min

Ingredients
- 1 apples, cored
- 1 cup apple juice
- 1 cup vanilla non-fat frozen yogurt
- 1/2 teaspoon cinnamon, ground
- 1 cup ice cube
- 1 scoop Collagen Boost, optional

Instructions
1. Place all of the ingredients in your blender, and blend until you get a creamy smoothie.

MORE VITAMIX SMOOTHIE

Nutrition: Cal 275; Fat 3 g; Carb 60 g; Protein 4 g
Serving 1; Cook time 10 min

Ingredients
- 1/2 cup blueberries, frozen
- 1/2 cup raspberries, frozen
- 1/2 cup red grapes
- 1/2 cup strawberries, frozen
- 1/2 cup vanilla nonfat frozen yogurt
- 1/2 cup water
- 1 cup ice

Instructions
1. Place all of the ingredients in your blender, and blend until you get a creamy smoothie.

VITAMIX BANANA RASPBERRY GREEN SMOOTHIE

Nutrition: Cal 236; Fat 3 g; Carb 140 g; Protein 4 g
Serving 1; Cook time 10 min

Ingredients
- 1 bananas, frozen, sliced
- 1 cup raspberries, frozen
- 1 cup romaine lettuce
- 1 cup spinach
- 1/2 cup almond milk, unsweetened
- 1 sprig mint, fresh scoop Collagen Boost, optional

Instructions
1. Place all of the ingredients in your blender, and blend until you get a creamy smoothie.

BEET POMEGRANATE CITRUS SMOOTHIE

Nutrition: Cal 179; Fat 3 g; Carb 75 g; Protein 4 g
Serving 1; Cook time 10 min

Ingredients
- 1/2 beets, raw
- 1/4 lemons, peeled
- 1 oranges, peeled
- 1 cup spinach
- 1 cup pomegranate juice
- 2 tbsp ginger, grated
- 1/2 cup parsley, Italian flat leaf
- 1 cup ice

Instructions
1. Place all of the ingredients in your blender, and blend until you get a creamy smoothie.

DETOX SMOOTHIE

Nutrition: Cal 160; Fat 3 g; Carb 39 g; Protein 4 g
Serving 1; Cook time 10 min

Ingredients
- ½ cup spinach
- ½ cup kale
- 1 cup water
- 1 cup mango
- ½ cup pineapple

Instructions
1. Place all of the ingredients in your blender, and blend until you get a creamy smoothie.

LEMON KALE PROTEIN

Nutrition: Cal 160; Fat 3 g; Carb 38 g; Protein 4 g
Serving 1; Cook time 10 min

Ingredients
- 1/2 lemon, peeled and seeded
- 1/2 frozen banana
- 1 cup kale
- 1/2 cup unsweetened almond milk

- 1 scoop plain plant-based protein powder
- 3 ice cubes
- Water to blend (optional)

Instructions
1. Place all of the ingredients in your blender, and blend until you get a creamy smoothie.

ENERGIZING ANTIOXIDANT SMOOTHIE

Nutrition: Cal 268; Fat 3 g; Carb 57 g; Protein 4 g
Serving 1; Cook time 10 min

Ingredients
- 2 oz pea protein powder
- 1 cup raw blueberries
- 1/2 small banana
- 1/2 cup unsweetened almond milk
- 1 cup chopped raw kale

Instructions
1. Place all of the ingredients in your blender, and blend until you get a creamy smoothie.

ISLAND GREEN SMOOTHIE

Nutrition: Cal 180; Fat 3 g; Carb 43 g; Protein 4 g
Serving 1; Cook time 10 min

Ingredients
- 1/2 frozen banana
- 1/2 cup frozen mango
- 1/2 cup frozen pineapple
- 2 cups spinach
- 1 cup kale
- 1 inch ginger
- 1/2 cup ice
- 1/4 cup water

Instructions
1. Place all of the ingredients in your blender, and blend until you get a creamy smoothie.

SUPERFOOD GREEN DETOX SMOOTHIE

Nutrition: Cal 181; Fat 3 g; Carb 26 g; Protein 4 g
Serving 1; Cook time 10 min

Ingredients
- 1 cup chopped Swiss chard about 5 leaves, without the stems
- 1/2 cup spinach
- 1 cup pomegranate seeds seeded, or juice with a citrus juicer as
- 1/4 avocado pit, and skin removed
- 3/4 cup coconat milk
- 1 tablespoon peeled and grated fresh ginger
- 3 Medjool dates pitted

Instructions
1. Place all of the ingredients in your blender, and blend until you get a creamy smoothie.

DELICIOUS ARUGULA SMOOTHIE

Nutrition: Cal 125; Fat 3 g; Carb 35 g; Protein 4 g
Serving 1; Cook time 10 min

Ingredients

- 1/2 cup fresh arugula
- 1 small banana, frozen*
- 1/2 green apple, cored and sliced into chunks
- 1 heaping tablespoon natural almond butter
- 1/2 tsp cinnamon
- 1 tablespoon raw honey
- 1/2 cup unsweetened vanilla almond milk
- 1 scoop collagen peptides (2 tablespoons) or vegan vanilla protein powder

Instructions
1. Place all of the ingredients in your blender, and blend until you get a creamy smoothie.

SWEETIE PEA GREEN SMOOTHIE

Nutrition: Cal 383; Fat 3 g; Carb 75 g; Protein 4 g
Serving 1; Cook time 10 min

Ingredients
- 1 cup sweet peas
- 1 banana
- 1/2 cup blueberries
- 1 cup almond milk
- 1 tablespoon chia seeds
- ½ teaspoon honey

Instructions
1. Place all of the ingredients in your blender, and blend until you get a creamy smoothie.

GREEN PROTEIN SMOOTHIE

Nutrition: Cal 237; Fat 11 g; Carb 33 g; Protein 4 g
Serving 1; Cook time 10 min

Ingredients
- 1/2 cup unsweetened almond milk
- 1 tablespoon almond butter
- 1 banana
- 2 cups baby spinach

Instructions
1. Place all of the ingredients in your blender, and blend until you get a creamy smoothie.

GLOWING GREEN SMOOTHIE

Nutrition: Cal 191; Fat 3 g; Carb 48 g; Protein 4 g
Serving 1; Cook time 10 min

Ingredients
- 1 kiwi peeled and quartered
- 1 banana
- ¼ cup pineapple
- celery stalks
- cups spinach
- 1 cup water

Instructions
1. Place all of the ingredients in your blender, and blend until you get a creamy smoothie.

APPLE BERRY SMOOTHIE

Nutrition: Cal 210; Fat 3 g; Carb 60g; Protein 4 g
Serving 1; Cook time 10 min

Ingredients
- 1 cup mixed berries like raspberries, strawberries, and blueberries
- 1 large apple cored and sliced
- 2 cups spinach
- 1 cup water

Instructions
1. Place all of the ingredients in your blender, and blend until you get a creamy smoothie.

PINEAPPLE BANANA SMOOTHIE

Nutrition: Cal 310; Fat 3 g; Carb 81 g; Protein 4 g
Serving 1; Cook time 10 min

Ingredients
- 1 cup pineapple
- 1 banana
- 1 apple
- 2 cups spinach
- 1 cup water

Instructions
1. Place all of the ingredients in your blender, and blend until you get a creamy smoothie.

PEACHES AND CREAM OATMEAL GREEN SMOOTHIE

Nutrition: Cal 331; Fat 3 g; Carb 46 g; Protein 4 g
Serving 1; Cook time 10 min

Ingredients
- 1 cup frozen peach slices
- 1 cup Greek yogurt I like unsweetened, but peach flavor is excellent here
- 1/4 cup oatmeal
- 1/4 teaspoon vanilla extract
- 1 cup almond milk
- 1 cup baby spinach

Instructions
1. Place all of the ingredients in your blender, and blend until you get a creamy smoothie.

BERRY DELICIOUS DETOX DIET SMOOTHIE

Nutrition: Cal 94; Fat 3 g; Carb 25 g; Protein 4 g
Serving 1; Cook time 10 min

Ingredients
- 1/2 cup strawberries
- 1/2 cup blueberries
- 1/4 cup raspberries
- 2 cups spinach

Instructions
1. Place all of the ingredients in your blender, and blend until you get a creamy smoothie.

KALE AND APPLE GREEN SMOOTHIE

Nutrition: Cal 148; Fat 3 g; Carb 17 g; Protein 4 g
Serving 1; Cook time 10 min

Ingredients
- 2/3 cup almond milk unsweetened
- 3/4 cup ice
- 1 1/2 cups kale chopped
- 1 stalk celery chopped
- 1/2 red or green apple cored and chopped
- 1 tbsp ground flax seed
- 1 teaspoon honey optiona

Instructions
1. Place all of the ingredients in your blender, and blend until you get a creamy smoothie.

KALE PINEAPPLE COCONUT SMOOTHIE

Nutrition: Cal 199; Fat 3 g; Carb 71 g; Protein 4 g
Serving 1; Cook time 10 min

Ingredients
- 1 banana
- 1 cup pineapple
- 1 cup coconut water
- 2 cups kale chopped

Instructions
1. Place all of the ingredients in your blender, and blend until you get a creamy smoothie.

KALE STRAWBERRY BANANA SMOOTHIE

Nutrition: Cal 358; Fat 3 g; Carb 62 g; Protein 4 g
Serving 1; Cook time 10 min

Ingredients
- 1 banana
- 1 cup 0% Greek yogurt
- 1 cup strawberries fresh or frozen
- 1 cup Kale chopped
- 1 cup ice

Instructions
1. Place all of the ingredients in your blender, and blend until you get a creamy smoothie.

AVOCADO DETOX SMOOTHIE

Nutrition: Cal 325; Fat 3 g; Carb 41 g; Protein 4 g
Serving 1; Cook time 10 min

Ingredients
- 1/2 cups water
- cups spinach or kale stemmed if using kale
- 1 apple cored, and sliced
- 1/2 avocado sliced or cubed

Instructions
1. Place all of the ingredients in your blender, and blend until you get a creamy smoothie.

LIVER DETOX GREEN SMOOTHIE

Nutrition: Cal 267 ; Fat 15; Carb 29 g; Protein 4 g
Serving 1; Cook time 10 min

Ingredients
- 1 cup unsweetened plant milk
- 1/2 ripe banana, frozen
- 1/3 cup frozen pineapple
- 1/4 ripe avocado
- handfuls baby spinach or baby kale
- 5–10 sprigs of fresh cilantro, stems removed
- 1/2 teaspoon ground cinnamon
- 1–2 scoops unsweetened protein powder (optional, for extra protein)

Instructions
1. Place all of the ingredients in your blender, and blend until you get a creamy smoothie.

BEETROOT SMOOTHIE

Nutrition: Cal 193; Fat 3 g; Carb 47 g; Protein 4 g
Serving 1; Cook time 10 min

Ingredients
- 1 pack of LeaderBrand beetroot
- 1 cup fresh raspberries
- 200ml fresh apple Juice

Instructions
1. Place all of the ingredients in your blender, and blend until you get a creamy smoothie.

METABOLISM BOOSTING BLUEBERRY SMOOTHIE

Nutrition: Cal 203; Fat 3 g; Carb 40 g; Protein 4 g
Serving 1; Cook time 10 min

Ingredients
- 2 tablespoon protein powder (scoops)
- 1/2 cup unsweetened almond milk (plain or vanilla or 1/2 cup canned full fat coconut milk)
- 1/2 cup ice cubes
- 1/2 cup blueberries (fresh or frozen)
- 1/4 cup baby spinach leaves (optional)
- 1 banana
- 1 tablespoon ground flaxseed or chia seeds

Instructions
1. Place all of the ingredients in your blender, and blend until you get a creamy smoothie.

EASY DETOX SMOOTHIE

Nutrition: Cal 198; Fat 3 g; Carb 51 g; Protein 4 g
Serving 1; Cook time 10 min

Ingredients
- 1/2 cup water (or orange juice)
- green apple
- 1/2 cup frozen pineapple chunks
- 1/2 frozen banana
- 1/2 inch fresh ginger , peeled and minced
- 1 cup fresh spinach
- 1 small handful fresh cilantro
- 1 tablespoon fresh lime juice

Instructions
1. Place all of the ingredients in your blender, and blend until you get a creamy smoothie.

EASY FLAX SEED SMOOTHIE

Nutrition: Cal 326; Fat 3 g; Carb 67 g; Protein 4 g
Serving 1; Cook time 10 min

Ingredients
- 1 cup water
- 1 large frozen banana
- 1 cup frozen mango
- 2 tablespoons ground flax seed
- 1 heaping cup fresh baby spinach (1 huge handful)
- 1/4 cup orange juice (optional; but so good!)
- 1/2 inch fresh ginger , peeled (optional)

Instructions
1. Place all of the ingredients in your blender, and blend until you get a creamy smoothie.

DETOX JUICE

Nutrition: Cal 183; Fat 1 g; Carb 49 g; Protein 4 g
Serving 1; Cook time 10 min

Ingredients
- English cucumber
- 1 head of celery (about 6 stalks)
- 1 small handful of Italian parsley
- 1 apple
- 1 small lemon (or half of a large one; no need to peel it)
- 1 inch knob of fresh ginger (no need to peel)

Instructions
1. Place all of the ingredients in your blender, and blend until you get a creamy smoothie.

SPIRULINA SMOOTHIE

Nutrition: Cal 284; Fat 3 g; Carb 69 g; Protein 4 g
Serving 1; Cook time 10 min

Ingredients
- 1 cup water
- 1/2 cucumber , peeled (to avoid bitterness)
- 1 frozen banana
- 1 cup mixed berries (frozen)
- 1 to 2 teaspoons spirulina powder (you can use up to 1 tablespoon)
- 1 Medjool date , pitted
- 1 large handful baby spinach

Instructions
1. Place all of the ingredients in your blender, and blend until you get a creamy smoothie.

BLUEBERRY DETOX SMOOTHIE

Nutrition: Cal 326; Fat 3 g; Carb 65 g; Protein 4 g
Serving 1; Cook time 10 min

Ingredients
- 1 cup frozen wild blueberries
- 1 small handful fresh cilantro leaves (see note)

- 1 frozen banana, cut into pieces for easy blending
- 1/4 avocado
- 1/2 cup orange juice
- 1/4 cup water

Instructions
1. Place all of the ingredients in your blender, and blend until you get a creamy smoothie.

APPLE, SPINACH, AND LIME SMOOTHIE

Nutrition: Cal 246; Fat 3 g; Carb 51 g; Protein 4 g
Serving 1; Cook time 10 min

Ingredients
- 1 small apple, chopped
- 1 tangerine, peeled
- 1 tablespoon lime juice
- 1/4 teaspoon powdered ginger
- 1 cup baby spinach leaves
- 1/2 cup plain non-fat Greek yogurt
- 1 tablespoon honey
- 1/2 cup ice

Instructions
1. Place all of the ingredients in your blender, and blend until you get a creamy smoothie.

BEST BEET SMOOTHIE

Nutrition: Cal 237; Fat 1 g; Carb 58 g; Protein 4 g
Serving 1; Cook time 10 min

Ingredients
- 1/2 cup fresh beet, chopped (I don't peel it)
- 1/2-inch piece fresh ginger (peeled, see note)
- 1/2 cup orange juice
- 1/2 cup water
- 1 frozen banana, cut into pieces
- 1 cup frozen strawberries

Instructions
1. Place all of the ingredients in your blender, and blend until you get a creamy smoothie.

BROCCOLI DETOX SMOOTHIE

Nutrition: Cal 237; Fat 3 g; Carb 58 g; Protein 4 g
Serving 2; Cook time 10 min

Ingredients
- 3/4 cup broccoli florets (chopped)
- 1 banana
- 1/2 cup pineapple cut in chunks
- 1/2 cup almond milk (use a milk of choice)
- 1/2 tspn flax seeds (optional)
- 1/2 tspn bee pollen (optional)

Instructions
1. Place all of the ingredients in your blender, and blend until you get a creamy smoothie.

BROCCOLI LEMON DETOX SMOOTHIE

Nutrition: Cal 133; Fat 3 g; Carb 52g; Protein 4 g
Serving 1; Cook time 10 min

Ingredients

- 130 g of broccoli
- 200 g of spinach shoots
- 30 cl of skimmed milk
- ½ lemon
- tablespoon of maple syrup

Instructions
1. Place all of the ingredients in your blender, and blend until you get a creamy smoothie.

CELERA SMOOTHIE

Nutrition: Cal 165; Fat 3 g; Carb 47 g; Protein 4 g
Serving 1; Cook time 10 min

Ingredients
- 1 cup almond milk
- 1/4 cup plain greek yogurt
- 2 cups spinach
- 1 celery stalk chopped
- 1 cup frozen pineapple
- 1 frozen banana
- 1 Tablespoon Honey
- chia seeds optional

Instructions
1. Place all of the ingredients in your blender, and blend until you get a creamy smoothie.

BEST GREEN SMOOTHIE

Nutrition: Cal 142; Fat 3 g; Carb 28 g; Protein 4 g
Serving 1; Cook time 10 min

Ingredients
- 1 green apple
- 1 green or yellow kiwi
- 1 handful of spinach - about 50g
- 1/4 squeezed lime or lemon juice
- 1/2 cup fruit - bananas and or pineapple about 100 g
- 1 cup almond milk or water, coconut water - about 220 - 250 ml
- 1/2 cup sliced cucumber - about 50 g
- 1 small piece of fresh ginger without the skin

Instructions
1. Place all of the ingredients in your blender, and blend until you get a creamy smoothie.

5-MINUTE SMOOTHIE

Nutrition: Cal 437 Fat 3 g; Carb 74 g; Protein 4 g
Serving 1; Cook time 10 min

Ingredients
- 2 cups baby spinach
- 1 grapefruit, peeled and cut into small pieces
- ¼ cup fresh parley, roughly chopped
- 1 cup orange juice, freshly squeezed
- juice of ½ lime, freshly squeezed
- juice of ½ lemon, freshly squeezed
- 4 tablespoons honey

Instructions

1. Place all of the ingredients in your blender, and blend until you get a creamy smoothie.

SIRTUIN GREEN DETOX SMOOTHIE

Nutrition: Cal 143; Fat 3 g; Carb 28 g; Protein 8 g
Serving 1; Cook time 10 min

Ingredients
- 1/2 apple ginger slices , (root)
- 1/2 cucumber
- 1/2 celery
- 1/2 of kale, (a handful)
- 1/2 lime juice, (half a lime)
- 1/2 cup of water
- parsley (handful)

Instructions
1. Place all of the ingredients in your blender, and blend until you get a creamy smoothie.

DETOX SIRT SMOOTHIE

Nutrition: Cal 101; Fat 3 g; Carb 21 g; Protein 4 g
Serving 1; Cook time 10 min

Ingredients
- 1/2 of sprouts
- 1/2 of arugula
- 1/2 of parsley
- 1/2 of celery
- 1 green apple
- Juice of half a Lemon
- 1/2tsp of Matcha green tea

Instructions
1. Place all of the ingredients in your blender, and blend until you get a creamy smoothie.

TROPICAL ISLAND GREEN SMOOTHIE

Nutrition: Cal 180; Fat 0 g; Carb 43 g; Protein 4 g
Serving 1; Cook time 10 min

Ingredients
- 1/2 teaspoon Spirulina powder
- cup Coconut water
- 1/2 Banana
- A few cuts of frozen Pineapple
- Less then a handful of sliced Mango
- 1/2 Kale
- 1/2 tbsp Ground ginger

Instructions
1. Place all of the ingredients in your blender, and blend until you get a creamy smoothie.

GREEN DETOX CUCUMBER SMOOTHIE

Nutrition: Cal 110; Fat 3 g; Carb 25 g; Protein 4 g
Serving 1; Cook time 10 min

Ingredients
- 1 cup freshly squeezed orange juice
- 1 medium size english cucumber diced and frozen
- a handful of seedless green grapes (cleaned)

Instructions

1. Place all of the ingredients in your blender, and blend until you get a creamy smoothie.

PINEAPPLE AND CUCUMBER DETOX SMOOTHIE

Nutrition: Cal 225; Fat 3 g; Carb 52 g; Protein 4 g
Serving 1; Cook time 10 min

Ingredients
- 2 cups chopped pineapple
- 1 medium cucumber
- 1 tsp lemon juice
- 3-4 mint leaves
- 1/2 cup green tea

Instructions
1. Place all of the ingredients in your blender, and blend until you get a creamy smoothie.

BLUEBERRY LIMON DETOX SMOOTHIE

Nutrition: Cal 111; Fat 3 g; Carb 19 g; Protein 4 g
Serving 1; Cook time 10 min

Ingredients
- 3 big oranges
- riped banana
- 1 cup frozen wild blueberries
- 1 cup cilantro leaves
- 1 cup parsley leaves
- 1 lemon

Instructions
1. Place all of the ingredients in your blender, and blend until you get a creamy smoothie.

SPINACH CUCUMBER SMOOTHIE

Nutrition: Cal 172; Fat 3 g; Carb 23 g; Protein 4 g
Serving 1; Cook time 10 min

Ingredients
- 1 apple (medium)
- 1 1/2 cup spinach , packed
- 1 cucumber
- 1 avocado
- cups almond milk
- 8 pitted dates

Instructions
1. Place all of the ingredients in your blender, and blend until you get a creamy smoothie.

DETOX CARROT & TURMERIC SMOOTHIE

Nutrition: Cal 121; Fat 2 g; Carb 24 g; Protein 4 g
Serving 1; Cook time 10 min

Ingredients
- 3-4 oranges
- new harvest medium carrot
- 1 medium golden apples
- piece of fresh ginger
- a small piece of fresh turmeric

Instructions
1. Place all of the ingredients in your blender, and blend until you get a creamy smoothie.

KALE SMOOTHIE

Nutrition: Cal 114; Fat 3 g; Carb 24 g; Protein 5 g
Serving 1; Cook time 10 min

Ingredients
- 3 cups kale stemmed
- 2 stalks celery roughly chopped
- 3 cups coconut water
- 1 green apple
- 1 tablespoon grated ginger
- 1 tablespoon Wholesome Allulose sweetener

Instructions
1. Place all of the ingredients in your blender, and blend until you get a creamy smoothie.

GREEN DETOX KETO SMOOTHIE

Nutrition: Cal 137; Fat 3 g; Carb 7 g; Protein 4 g
Serving 1; Cook time 10 min

Ingredients
- 1 handful / kale
- 1/4 cup handful fresh mint leaves, picked
- 1/2 avocado
- 1/4 fennel or 1 celery stick
- 1/4 small cucumber
- 1 tablespoon protein powder unsweetened
- 1 cup almond milk unsweetened
- 1 tablespoon almond butter
- 1/2 lemon, juiced

Instructions
1. Place all of the ingredients in your blender, and blend until you get a creamy smoothie.

PURPLE POWER DETOX SMOOTHIE

Nutrition: Cal 272; Fat 3 g; Carb 16 g; Protein 4 g
Serving 1; Cook time 10 min

Ingredients
- 1 cup frozen blueberries
- 1/2 large beet (or 1 small/medium beet)
- 1 ripe banana (fresh or frozen – add extra liquid if frozen)
- 1/4-1/2 cup unsweetened coconut milk
- 1 cup chopped kale (leaves removed from stem)
- TBSP orange juice

Instructions
1. Place all of the ingredients in your blender, and blend until you get a creamy smoothie.

GREEN DETOX SMOOTHIE FOR A HEALTHIER BREAKFAST

Nutrition: Cal 201; Fat 3 g; Carb 22 g; Protein 4 g
Serving 1; Cook time 10 min

Ingredients
- 3 kale leaves
- 1 cup coconut milk or coconut water for a skinnier version
- 1/2 cup pineapple cut in pieces or 1 cup pineapple juice
- 1 tsp cinnamon
- 1 tbsp honey
- 2-3 ice cubes optional

Instructions
1. Place all of the ingredients in your blender, and blend until you get a creamy smoothie.

GOLDEN DETOX SMOOTHIE

Nutrition: Cal 472; Fat 3 g; Carb 105 g; Protein 4 g
Serving 1; Cook time 10 min

Ingredients
- 1 banana
- 1 1Tbsp honey greek yogurt
- 1 carrot peeled and diced
- 1/2 c. fresh pineapple
- 1/2 c. orange juice fresh squeezed
- 1/2 c. water

Instructions
1. Place all of the ingredients in your blender, and blend until you get a creamy smoothie.

MIXED BERRY DETOX SMOOTHIE

Nutrition: Cal 317; Fat 3 g; Carb 52 g; Protein 4 g
Serving 1; Cook time 10 min

Ingredients
- 3/4 cup unsweetened almond milk
- 1 cup mixed berries frozen
- 1/2 cup fresh cranberries
- 1/4 cup baby spinach
- 1 banana chopped
- 1 tablespoon flax seeds
- 1 tablespoon almond butter
- the juice of half lime
- 1/4 teaspoon cayenne pepper
- 1 teaspoon chia seeds

Instructions
1. Place all of the ingredients in your blender, and blend until you get a creamy smoothie.

GREEN MIX DETOX SMOOTHIE

Nutrition: Cal 324; Fat 9 g; Carb 63 g; Protein 4 g
Serving 1; Cook time 10 min

Ingredients
- 2 cups kale, de-stemmed (or spinach, chard etc.)
- 1/2 english cucumber, chopped
- 2 stalks celery, chopped
- 1 small lemon, peel removed
- 1 ripe banana, frozen
- 1 cup pineapple (frozen)
- tablespoons chia seeds
- 1/2–1 teaspoon spirulina powder (depending on preference)
- 1 cup unsweetened almond milk
- 1 cup cold, filtered water
- handful of ice (optional)

Instructions
1. Place all of the ingredients in your blender, and blend until you get a creamy smoothie.

CLEANSE & DETOX SMOOTHIE

Nutrition: Cal 189; Fat 3 g; Carb 39 g; Protein 4 g
Serving 1; Cook time 10 min

Ingredients
- 1 apple organic
- 1 lemon juiced
- 1 cup kale
- 1 celery stalk
- 1/3 cup flat-leaf parsley or cilantro
- 1 tablespoon ground flaxseed or chia seeds
- 1/4 teaspoon ground cinnamon
- 1 1/4 cups chilled water

Instructions
1. Place all of the ingredients in your blender, and blend until you get a creamy smoothie.

NATURALLY SWEET GREEN DETOX JUICE

Nutrition: Cal 66; Fat 3 g; Carb 16 g; Protein 4 g
Serving 1; Cook time 10 min

Ingredients
- 2 cups packed baby spinach leaves
- Handful parsley leaves and stems
- 1 medium green apple, rinsed with core removed
- 1 large seedless (hothouse or English) cucumber, rinsed
- 1-inch length piece fresh ginger, scrubbed clean
- 1 medium lemon

Instructions
1. Place all of the ingredients in your blender, and blend until you get a creamy smoothie.

DETOX SPINACH GREEN SMOOTHIE

Nutrition: Cal 168; Fat 3 g; Carb 44 g; Protein 4 g
Serving 1; Cook time 10 min

Ingredients
- 2 bananas
- 1 apple
- 1 cup baby spinach
- 1 lemon
- 1 cup water, or as needed

Instructions
1. Place all of the ingredients in your blender, and blend until you get a creamy smoothie.

TURMERIC PERSIMMON SMOOTHIE {VEGAN}

Nutrition: Cal 168; Fat 3 g; Carb 43 g; Protein 4 g
Serving 1; Cook time 10 min

Ingredients
- 4 soft persimmons
- 2 small bananas
cup water or more as needed
- 1/4 ts cinnamon
- 1/4 ts turmeric
- Juice of half a lemon
- 2tbs natural plant-based yogurt
- cacao nibs

Instructions
1. Place all of the ingredients in your blender, and blend until you get a creamy smoothie.

VEGAN PROBIOTIC BERRY SMOOTHIE

Nutrition: Cal 189; Fat 3 g; Carb 44 g; Protein 4 g
Serving 1; Cook time 10 min

Ingredients
- 1 apple
- 1 pear
- 1/2 cup frozen blueberries
- 1/2 cup frozen raspberries
- 1 cup frozen strawberries
- 1 cup coconut yogurt
- 1 cup water

Instructions
1. Place all of the ingredients in your blender, and blend until you get a creamy smoothie.

ANTIOXIDANT BLACKBERRY KALE SMOOTHIE {VEGAN}

Nutrition: Cal 141; Fat 3 g; Carb 42 g; Protein 4 g
Serving 1; Cook time 10 min

Ingredients
- 3 peaches
- 4 leaves purple kale, stems removed
- 1/2 cup blackberries, fresh or frozen
- 1/3 cup blueberries, fresh or frozen
- 2 tbs lemon juice
- 1 cup water, or as needed
- mint leaves (optional for decoration)

Instructions
1. Place all of the ingredients in your blender, and blend until you get a creamy smoothie.

SUPER GREEN AVOCADO SMOOTHIE

Nutrition: Cal 167; Fat 6 g; Carb 28 g; Protein 4 g
Serving 1; Cook time 10 min

Ingredients
- 1 banana
- 1/2 avocado
- 1 cup baby spinach
- 1/2 cup plain coconut yogurt
- 1/2 lemon, juice
- 1 cup water

Instructions
1. Place all of the ingredients in your blender, and blend until you get a creamy smoothie.

AIP GREEN DETOX SMOOTHIE

Nutrition: Cal 174; Fat 0 g; Carb 42 g; Protein 4 g
Serving 1; Cook time 10 min

Ingredients
- 2 oz of kale, roughly chopped
- 1 small Granny Smith apple (150 g), core removed and roughly chopped
- oz (100 g or roughly 5 stalks) of celery, roughly chopped

- 1 lemon, rind and pips removed and diced small
- generous handful mint leaves
- 1 thumb-size piece ginger, peeled and roughly diced

Instructions
1. Place all of the ingredients in your blender, and blend until you get a creamy smoothie.

AIP TROPICAL SMOOTHIE

Nutrition: Cal 125 ; Fat 3 g; Carb 25 g; Protein 4 g
Serving 1; Cook time 10 min

Ingredients
- 1 banana peeled and diced
- 6 oz of coconut water
- 14 oz of pineapple chunks
- 2 Tablespoons of full-fat coconut milk (from a can)

Instructions
1. Place all of the ingredients in your blender, and blend until you get a creamy smoothie.

GREEN APPLE DETOX SMOOTHIE

Nutrition: Cal 266; Fat 3 g; Carb 65 g; Protein 4 g
Serving 1; Cook time 10 min

Ingredients
- 2 cups frozen kale
- 1/2 cups coconut water
- 1-2 Tbsp grated ginger (or 1/2 tsp ginger powder)
- 1 medium green apple
- 2-3 stalks celery
- 1cups frozen pineapple
- 1 medium banana
- 1/2 medium lemon, juiced

Instructions
1. Place all of the ingredients in your blender, and blend until you get a creamy smoothie.

HYDRATING PARSLEY DETOX SMOOTHIE

Nutrition: Cal 178; Fat 3 g; Carb 45 g; Protein 4 g
Serving 1; Cook time 10 min

Ingredients
- 1 cup parsley
- 1 cup chopped cucumber
- 1/2 juice of lemon
- 2 inches fresh ginger
- 1 apple
- 1 cup water

Instructions
1. Place all of the ingredients in your blender, and blend until you get a creamy smoothie.

CHLORELLA DETOX SMOOTHIE

Nutrition: Cal 206; Fat 3 g; Carb 50 g; Protein 4 g
Serving 1; Cook time 10 min

Ingredients
- 1 cup kale or spinach stems removed
- 1/2 banana frozen
- 3/4 cup pineapple chunks frozen
- 1/2 inch fresh ginger skin peeled off (this ingredient optional)
- 1/2 teaspoon chlorella powder or the powder from 2 capsules

Instructions
1. Place all of the ingredients in your blender, and blend until you get a creamy smoothie.

LIME SMOOTHIE

Nutrition: Cal 125; Fat 3 g; Carb 47 g; Protein 4 g
Serving 1; Cook time 10 min

Ingredients
- 1/3 cup filtered water
- 1 banana (peeled)
- 1 lime (peeled)
- 1/3 cucumber
- leaves kale
- 1 handful parsley
- 1-2 cups ice

Instructions
1. Place all of the ingredients in your blender, and blend until you get a creamy smoothie.

SUPER FOOD SMOOTHIE

Nutrition: Cal 145; Fat 3 g; Carb 51 g; Protein 4 g
Serving 1; Cook time 10 min

Ingredients
- 8 frozen kale leaves
- 2 frozen spinach leaf blocks
- 4/3 coconut milk
- 2/4 cup pineapple juice
- 2 tsp kent squeezy honey
- 1 tsp cinnamon ground

Instructions
1. Place all of the ingredients in your blender, and blend until you get a creamy smoothie.

CHERRY SMOOTHIE

Nutrition: Cal 337; Fat 3 g; Carb 28 g; Protein 8 g
Serving 1; Cook time 10 min

Ingredients
- 1 cup frozen cherries
- 1/2 large papaya seeds and rind removed
- 1 large banana
- 1/2 inch ginger root grated
- 1/2 cups coconut almond milk or plain almond milk will do
- 1 tbsp pumpkin seeds raw
- 2 tbsp flax seeds ground

Instructions
1. Place all of the ingredients in your blender, and blend until you get a creamy smoothie.

CHERRY BEET SMOOTHIE FOR DETOX AND GUT HEALTH

Nutrition: Cal 310; Fat 11 g; Carb 28 g; Protein 4 g
Serving 1; Cook time 10 min

Ingredients
- 1 cup frozen cherries
- 1/4 banana
- 1/4 cup frozen pomegranate
- 1/4 cup chopped raw beet
- 1 tbsp sunflower seeds
- 1 tbsp pumkin seeds
- 1/2 cup water

Instructions
1. Place all of the ingredients in your blender, and blend until you get a creamy smoothie.

CRANBERRY CHERRY SMOOTHIE

Nutrition: Cal 285; Fat 3 g; Carb 28 g; Protein 10 g
Serving 1; Cook time 10 min

Ingredients
- 1 cup almond milk
- 1 cup frozen pitted sweet cherries
- 1/2 cup ice
- 1 ripe banana
- 1/4 cup cranberries (fresh OR frozen)
- 1 tablespoon chia seeds
- 1/4 inch slice ginger root

Instructions
1. Place all of the ingredients in your blender, and blend until you get a creamy smoothie.

SOUR CHERRY AND POMEGRANATE DETOX SMOOTHIE

Nutrition: Cal 259; Fat 3 g; Carb 62 g; Protein 4 g
Serving 1; Cook time 10 min

Ingredients
- 1/2 cup pineapple juice
- 1/2 banana
- Arils from 1/2 a pomegranate (about 1/2 a cup)
- 1 cup frozen dark sour cherries

Instructions
1. Place all of the ingredients in your blender, and blend until you get a creamy smoothie.

PINEAPPLE DETOX SMOOTHIE

Nutrition: Cal 123; Fat 3 g; Carb 31 g; Protein 4 g
Serving 1; Cook time 10 min

Ingredients
- cup fresh pineapple chunks
- 1 cucumber, peeled
- stalks of celery (optional - see notes)
- 1 lemon, peel cut off
- 1-2" piece of fresh ginger, peeled
- 1 cup frozen banana chunks
- 10 oz bag of frozen peach slices
- cups of ice

Instructions
1. Place all of the ingredients in your blender, and blend until you get a creamy smoothie.

WATERMELON DETOX WATER RECIPE

Nutrition: Cal 54; Fat 3 g; Carb 28 g; Protein 1 g
Serving 1; Cook time 10 min

Ingredients
- 1/2 cucumber, sliced
- 1 small lemon, sliced
- 1 1/2 cups cut up watermelon
- 2 cups filtered water
- 1 cup ice

Instructions
1. Place all of the ingredients in your blender, and blend until you get a creamy smoothie.

MANGO SMOOTHIE

Nutrition: Cal 297; Fat 3 g; Carb 70 g; Protein 4 g
Serving 1; Cook time 10 min

Ingredients
- 2 cups ripe mango chunks (or frozen)
- 2-3 Tablespoons fresh lime juice
- 2 cups unsweetened coconut water
- Pinch of cayenne powder

Instructions
1. Place all of the ingredients in your blender, and blend until you get a creamy smoothie.

MANGO GREEN TEA DETOX SMOOTHIE

Nutrition: Cal 65; Fat 3 g; Carb 11 g; Protein 4 g
Serving 1; Cook time 10 min

Ingredients
- 3 Green Tea Bags
- 1 Cup Hot Water
- 1 Cup Frozen Mango
- 1/2 Cup Frozen Pineapple
- 1 Cup Fresh Kale

Instructions
1. Place all of the ingredients in your blender, and blend until you get a creamy smoothie.

PINEAPPLE MANGO DETOX SMOOTHIE

Nutrition: Cal 54 ; Fat 3 g; Carb 14 g; Protein 4 g
Serving 1; Cook time 10 min

Ingredients
- 1 cup Pineapple
- 1/2 cup Mango
- 1 inch Ginger
- leaves of Mint
- 1/2 lime
- 1 tbsp Sugar (optional)
- 1/2 cup Water

Instructions
1. Place all of the ingredients in your blender, and blend until you get a creamy smoothie.

MANGO BANANA CELERY DETOX SMOOTHIE

Nutrition: Cal 156; Fat 3 g; Carb 28 g; Protein 10 g
Serving 1; Cook time 10 min

Ingredients
- 2 Cups Mango Use frozen mango chunks.
- 2 Medium Banana
- 2 Cups Celery Use chopped celery stalks.
- 1 Cup Cilantro
- 1/2 Lime Take half lime juice to boost antioxidants.
- Cups Water

Instructions
1. Place all of the ingredients in your blender, and blend until you get a creamy smoothie.

MANGO GINGER DETOX SMOOTHIE

Nutrition: Cal 262 ; Fat 3 g; Carb 28 g; Protein 11 g
Serving 1; Cook time 10 min

Ingredients
- 1 cup non-dairy milk
- 1 large banana sliced
- 1 cup frozen mango
- 1 tbsp. lemon juice
- tablespoons hemp hearts
- 1-2 tablespoon maple syrup
- 1 tsp. freshly ground ginger
- 1/2 teaspoon turmeric

Instructions
1. Place all of the ingredients in your blender, and blend until you get a creamy smoothie.

SPRING CLEANING MANGO DETOX SMOOTHIE

Nutrition: Cal 267; Fat 3 g; Carb 35 g; Protein 4 g
Serving 1; Cook time 10 min

Ingredients
- 2 cups fresh or frozen mango
- 1 cup ripe pineapple
- 1 cup freshly pressed orange juice
- 1/2 lemon, juiced
- 1 tsp. turmeric powder or 2 inches fresh turmeric root
- 1 tbsp. chia seeds
- 1 tsp. maca powder
- 1 small piece ginger root

Instructions
1. Place all of the ingredients in your blender, and blend until you get a creamy smoothie.

SKIN DETOX GREEN SMOOTHIE

Nutrition: Cal 167; Fat 3 g; Carb 35 g; Protein 7 g
Serving 1; Cook time 10 min

Ingredients
- 5 ripe kiwi
- 1 lime, juiced
- sprigs of mint
- 2 green apples
- 2 ripe spotty bananas

Instructions
1. Place all of the ingredients in your blender, and blend until you get a creamy smoothie.

MANGO LIME GREEN SMOOTHIE

Nutrition: Cal 204; Fat 3 g; Carb 51 g; Protein 4 g
Serving 1; Cook time 10 min

Ingredients
- 3 cups ripe mango
- 1cup packed kale
- 1 cup packed spinach
- medjool dates, pitted
- 1 celery stalk
- 1 cup coconut water or regular filtered water
- 1 inch ginger root

Instructions
1. Place all of the ingredients in your blender, and blend until you get a creamy smoothie.

DETOX GLOWING SKIN SMOOTHIE

Nutrition: Cal 288; Fat 3 g; Carb 28 g; Protein 4 g
Serving 1; Cook time 10 min

Ingredients
- 1 small banana (add just 1/2 if you're watching sugar)
- 2 cups fresh kale or baby spinach (I use 50/50)
- 1 cup pomegranate juice (fresh or bottled)
- 1/2 cup greek yogurt
- 1/2 cup blueberries (I use berries that I froze)
- 1/2 cup water or ice cubes

Instructions
1. Place all of the ingredients in your blender, and blend until you get a creamy smoothie.

KIWI DETOX SMOOTHIE

Nutrition: Cal 445; Fat 3 g; Carb 66 g; Protein 4 g
Serving 1; Cook time 10 min

Ingredients
- 1 peach peeled and sliced
- 1 kiwi peeled and sliced
- 1 frozen banana peeled and sliced
- 1 cup spinach
- ½ avocado peeled
- Juice of a lemon or lime
- ¼ cup unsweetened almond milk
- ¼ cup coconut water
- Grated ginger optional
- 1 scoop protein powder optional
- Maple syrup to taste

Instructions
1. Place all of the ingredients in your blender, and blend until you get a creamy smoothie.

SPRING DETOX - SMOOTHIE

Nutrition: Cal 310; Fat 3 g; Carb 52 g; Protein 7 g
Serving 1; Cook time 10 min

Ingredients
- 1 cup green tea chilled
- 1 cup cilantro loosely packed
- 1 cup kale loosely packed organic baby, or another baby green
- 1 cup cucumber
- 1 cup pineapple
- 1 lemon
- 1 tbsp fresh ginger grated
- 1/2 avocado

Instructions
1. Place all of the ingredients in your blender, and blend until you get a creamy smoothie.

SUPER ENERGY DETOX SMOOTHIE

Nutrition: Cal 253; Fat 3 g; Carb 64g; Protein 4 g
Serving 1; Cook time 10 min

Ingredients
- 1 apple
- 1 grapefruit
- 1 kiwi
- ice cubes or even better-shaved

Instructions
1. Place all of the ingredients in your blender, and blend until you get a creamy smoothie.

ULTIMATE GREEN DETOX SMOOTHIE (DAIRY FREE, VEGAN)

Nutrition: Cal 156; Fat 3 g; Carb 26 g; Protein 4 g
Serving 1; Cook time 10 min

Ingredients
- 2 Cups Organic Green Tea
- 1 Cup Organic Kale
- 1 Cup Organic Baby Spinach
- Sprigs Organic Mint
- 1 Organic Kiwi
- 1 Frozen Organic Fairtrade Bananas

Instructions
1. Place all of the ingredients in your blender, and blend until you get a creamy smoothie.

GREEN APPLE CUCUMBER DETOX SMOOTHIE

Nutrition: Cal 80; Fat 0g; Carb 18 g; Protein 4 g
Serving 1; Cook time 10 min

Ingredients
- 1 cup packed kale leaves, stems removed
- 1 cup packed spinach leaves
- Juice of 1/2 lemon
- 1 Granny Smith apple, cored and diced (approx. 1 and 1/4 cup)
- 1/2 cucumber, diced
- 1/2 teaspoon honey
- 1/2 cup water
- ice cubes

Instructions
1. Place all of the ingredients in your blender, and blend until you get a creamy smoothie.

CRANBERRY APPLE DETOX SMOOTHIE

Nutrition: Cal 292; Fat 3 g; Carb 44 g; Protein 4 g
Serving 1; Cook time 10 min

Ingredients
- 1 apple cored with peel left on
- 1 cup frozen cranberries
- 1/3 cup vanilla protein powder
- 1/2 cup unsweetened almond milk
- 1 tsp cinnamon

Instructions
1. Place all of the ingredients in your blender, and blend until you get a creamy smoothie.

LOW CARB CUCUMBER GREEN TEA DETOX SMOOTHIE

Nutrition: Cal 64 Fat 3 g; Carb 28 g; Protein 1 g
Serving 1; Cook time 10 min

Ingredients
- 8 ounces water
- 2 teaspoon Match Green Tea powder
- 1 cup cucumber sliced
- 1 avocado
- 1 teaspoon lemon juice
- 1/2 teaspoon lemon liquid stevia
- 1/2 cup ice

Instructions
1. Place all of the ingredients in your blender, and blend until you get a creamy smoothie.

CLEANSE & DETOX SMOOTHIE: DAIRY, SUGAR & GLUTEN FREE

Nutrition: Cal 194; Fat 3 g; Carb 34g; Protein 4 g
Serving 1; Cook time 10 min

Ingredients
- 1 apple cored [green preferred] or 1 green pear
- 1 cup spinach
- 1 stalk celery
- ½ cucumber
- ½ cup almond milk unsweetened
- 1 tablespoon flax seed
- juice of 1 lemon
- 1 ½ cup ice
- droppers liquid lemon stevia or plain

Instructions
1. Place all of the ingredients in your blender, and blend until you get a creamy smoothie.

BLUEBERRY BANANA DETOX SMOOTHIE

Nutrition: Cal 300; Fat 3 g; Carb 44 g; Protein 4 g
Serving 1; Cook time 10 min

Ingredients
- 1/2 cup Blueberries fresh or frozen
- 1/2 Banana
- 1/2 tbsp Coconut Oil
- 1 tsp Flax Seeds
- 6 ounces Water more if smoothie is too thick
- 1 tsp Honey more if you like it sweet

Instructions
1. Place all of the ingredients in your blender, and blend until you get a creamy smoothie.

HEALTHY GRAPEFRUIT GINGER DETOX SMOOTHIE

Nutrition: Cal 483; Fat 1 g; Carb 113 g; Protein 4 g
Serving 1; Cook time 10 min

Ingredients
- 1 cup grapefruit (1 medium grapefruit)
- 1/2 large carrot
- 1/2 cup frozen pineapple
- 1/2 cup greek yogurt
- Medjool dates
- 1 tbsp fresh ginger

Instructions
1. Place all of the ingredients in your blender, and blend until you get a creamy smoothie.

GRAPEFRUIT DETOX SMOOTHIE

Nutrition: Cal 125; Fat 3 g; Carb 27g; Protein 10 g
Serving 1; Cook time 10 min

Ingredients
- Juice from 2 Grapefruits
- 1 Cup Frozen Mango
- 1 Cup Frozen Pineapple
- 2-3 Fresh Spearmint Leaves
- 2-3 Ice Cubes
- Water to thin if needed

Instructions
1. Place all of the ingredients in your blender, and blend until you get a creamy smoothie.

GRAPEFRUIT, STRAWBERRY & SPINACH DETOX SMOOTHIE

Nutrition: Cal 196; Fat 1 g; Carb 28 g; Protein 47 g
Serving 1; Cook time 10 min

Ingredients
- 1 large pink grapefruit
- 100 g strawberries
- 1 handful baby spinach leaves
- 100 ml orange juice

Instructions
1. Place all of the ingredients in your blender, and blend until you get a creamy smoothie.

<u>Green Smoothie</u>

SMOOTHIE WITH BANANA AND HONEY ON MILK

Nutrition: Cal 192; Fat 7 g; Carb 30 g; Protein 4 g
Serving 1; Cook time 10 min

Ingredients
- 2 c. baby spinach
- 1 c. frozen pineapple chunks
- 1 c. light coconut milk
- 1 banana, sliced and frozen
- 1 tsp. grated lime zest
- 1 tbsp. lime juice

Instructions
1. Place all of the ingredients in your blender, and blend until you get a creamy smoothie.

MILK AND HONEY SMOOTHIE

Nutrition: Cal 124; Fat 3 g; Carb 26 g; Protein 2 g
Serving 1; Cook time 10 min

Ingredients
- 1,5 cups unsweetened almond milk
- 1 medium Kirby cucumber (peeled and sliced)
- 1 cup seedless green grapes
- medium stalks celery (peeled and sliced)
- 1 Tbsp honey

Instructions
1. Place all of the ingredients in your blender, and blend until you get a creamy smoothie.

STRAWBERRY-BANANA GREEN SMOOTHIE

Nutrition: Cal 318; Fat 3 g; Carb 51 g; Protein 19 g
Serving 1; Cook time 10 min

Ingredients
- 1 medium banana
- 1 cup baby spinach
- 1/2 cup low-fat plain Greek yogurt
- 1/2 cup nonfat milk
- 6 frozen strawberries
- 1 tablespoon flaxseeds

Instructions
1. Place all of the ingredients in your blender, and blend until you get a creamy smoothie.

GREEN PINEAPPLE COCONUT SMOOTHIE

Nutrition: Cal 192; Fat 3 g; Carb 30 g; Protein 4 g
Serving 1; Cook time 10 min

Ingredients
- 2 c. baby spinach
- 1 c. frozen pineapple chunks
- 1 c. light coconut milk
- 1 banana, sliced and frozen
- 1 tsp. grated lime zest
- 1 tbsp. lime juice

Instructions
1. Place all of the ingredients in your blender, and blend until you get a creamy smoothie.

SPINACH, PEANUT BUTTER & BANANA SMOOTHIE

Nutrition: Cal 324; Fat 3 g; Carb 44 g; Protein 4 g
Serving 1; Cook time 10 min

Ingredients
- 1 cup plain kefir
- 1 tablespoon peanut butter
- 1 cup spinach
- 1 frozen banana
- 1 tablespoon honey

Instructions
1. Place all of the ingredients in your blender, and blend until you get a creamy smoothie.

SPINACH-AVOCADO SMOOTHIE

Nutrition: Cal 357 ; Fat 8 g; Carb 57 g; Protein 4 g
Serving 1; Cook time 10 min

Ingredients
- 1 cup nonfat plain yogurt
- 1 cup fresh spinach
- 1 frozen banana
- 1/4 avocado
- 2 tablespoons water
- 1 teaspoon honey

Instructions
1. Place all of the ingredients in your blender, and blend until you get a creamy smoothie.

PINEAPPLE GREEN SMOOTHIE

Nutrition: Cal 297; Fat 3 g; Carb 54 g; Protein 4 g
Serving 1; Cook time 10 min

Ingredients
- 1/2 cup unsweetened almond milk
- 1/3 cup nonfat plain Greek yogurt
- 1 cup baby spinach
- 1 cup frozen banana slices (about 1 medium banana)
- 1/2 cup frozen pineapple chunks
- 1 tablespoon chia seeds
- 1-2 teaspoons pure maple syrup or honey

Instructions
1. Place all of the ingredients in your blender, and blend until you get a creamy smoothie.

MANGO & SPINACH SMOOTHIE

Nutrition: Cal 210; Fat 2 g; Carb 30 g; Protein 4 g
Serving 1; Cook time 10 min

Ingredients
- 1/2 cups baby spinach
- 1 cup frozen mango chunks
- 1/4 cup plain or vanilla low-fat Greek yogurt
- 1 cup unsweetened vanilla almond milk or other nondairy milk

Instructions
1. Place all of the ingredients in your blender, and blend until you get a creamy smoothie.

TROPICAL GREEN SMOOTHIE

Nutrition: Cal 300; Fat 3 g; Carb 28 g; Protein 20 g
Serving 1; Cook time 10 min

Ingredients
- 1/2 frozen banana
- 1/2 cup frozen mango
- 1 cup almond coconut milk blend
- 1-2 cups baby spinach
- 1 scoop plant-based vanilla protein powder
- 1/2 Tablespoon chia seeds
- 1 teaspoon unsweetened shredded coconut + more for topping

Instructions
1. Place all of the ingredients in your blender, and blend until you get a creamy smoothie.

REALLY GREEN SMOOTHIE

Nutrition: Cal 343; Fat 3 g; Carb 54 g; Protein 4 g
Serving 1; Cook time 10 min

Ingredients
- 1 large ripe banana
- 1 cup packed baby kale or coarsely chopped mature kale
- 1 cup unsweetened vanilla almond milk
- ¼ ripe avocado
- 1 tablespoon chia seeds
- 2 teaspoons honey
- 1 cup ice cubes

Instructions
1. Place all of the ingredients in your blender, and blend until you get a creamy smoothie.

JASON MRAZ'S AVOCADO GREEN SMOOTHIE

Nutrition: Cal 307; Fat 3 g; Carb 40 g; Protein 4 g
Serving 1; Cook time 10 min

Ingredients
- 1/4 cups cold unsweetened almond milk or coconut milk beverage
- 1 ripe avocado
- 1 ripe banana
- 1 sweet apple, such as Honeycrisp, sliced
- 1/2 large or 1 small stalk celery, chopped
- 2 cups lightly packed kale leaves or spinach
- 1 1-inch piece peeled fresh ginger
- 8 ice cubes

Instructions
1. Place all of the ingredients in your blender, and blend until you get a creamy smoothie.

GOOD GREEN TEA SMOOTHIE

Nutrition: Cal 142; Fat 3 g; Carb 28 g; Protein 4 g
Serving 1; Cook time 10 min

Ingredients
- 3 cups frozen white grapes
- 2 packed cups baby spinach
- 1/2 cups strong brewed green tea (see Tip), cooled
- 1 medium ripe avocado
- 2 teaspoons honey

Instructions
1. Place all of the ingredients in your blender, and blend until you get a creamy smoothie.

GREEN PINA COLADA SMOOTHIE

Nutrition: Cal 324; Fat 3 g; Carb 35 g; Protein 4 g
Serving 1; Cook time 10 min

Ingredients
- 1 cup nonfat plain Greek yogurt
- 1 cup frozen pineapple
- 1 cup kale or baby spinach
- 1/3 cup "lite" coconut milk (see Tip)
- 1/2 teaspoon vanilla extract

Instructions
1. Place all of the ingredients in your blender, and blend until you get a creamy smoothie.

ALL GREENS SMOOTHIE

Nutrition: Cal 270; Fat 3 g; Carb 52, g; Protein 4 g
Serving 1; Cook time 10 min

Ingredients
- 1 banana, frozen
- 1 pear, chopped
- 1 apple, chopped
- 1/4 cup spinach
- 1/4 cup watercress
- 1 cup unsweetened almond milk
- 1 kiwi, chopped
- 1/2 green apple, chopped
- tablespoons pumpkin seeds
- tablespoons unsweetened coconut flakes

Instructions
1. Place all of the ingredients in your blender, and blend until you get a creamy smoothie.

SPINACH SMOOTHIE

Nutrition: Cal 183; Fat 3 g; Carb 39 g; Protein 4 g
Serving 1; Cook time 10 min

Ingredients
- 1/2 cups baby spinach
- 1 small banana, sliced
- 1 cup frozen strawberries
- 2/3 cup unsweetened vanilla coconut milk or other nondairy milk

Instructions
1. Place all of the ingredients in your blender, and blend until you get a creamy smoothie.

3-INGREDIENT TROPICAL GREENS SMOOTHIE

Nutrition: Cal 229; Fat 3 g; Carb 28 g; Protein 11 g
Serving 1; Cook time 10 min

Ingredients
- (32-ounce) bag frozen tropical fruit medley
- 4 cups fresh baby spinach

- 4 cups reduced-fat milk or nondairy alternative, divided

Instructions
1. Place all of the ingredients in your blender, and blend until you get a creamy smoothie.

PINEAPPLE SPINACH SMOOTHIE

Nutrition: Cal 151; Fat 3 g; Carb 35 g; Protein 4 g
Serving 1; Cook time 10 min

Ingredients
- 1/4 cup pineapple juice
- 1/4 cup water
- 2 cups baby spinach
- 1/2 cup frozen mango chunks
- 1/2 cup frozen pineapple chunks

Instructions
1. Place all of the ingredients in your blender, and blend until you get a creamy smoothie.

GREEN SMOOTHIE

Nutrition: Cal 213; Fat 3 g; Carb 49 g; Protein 4 g
Serving 1; Cook time 10 min

Ingredients
- 2 ripe medium bananas
- 1 ripe pear or apple, peeled if desired, chopped
- 2 cups chopped kale leaves, tough stems removed
- 1/2 cup cold orange juice
- 1/2 cup cold water

Instructions
1. Place all of the ingredients in your blender, and blend until you get a creamy smoothie.

STRAWBERRY GREEN GODDESS SMOOTHIE

Nutrition: Cal 270; Fat 3 g; Carb 52 g; Protein 4 g
Serving 1; Cook time 10 min

Ingredients
- 1/2 ripe strawberries, hulled
- 1/2 baby spinach
- 1 small avocado, halved and the flesh scooped out
- 1/2 cup pot bio yogurt
- 2 small oranges, juiced, plus ½ tsp finely grated zest

Instructions
1. Place all of the ingredients in your blender, and blend until you get a creamy smoothie.

CLEANSING APPLE AVOCADO SMOOTHIE

Nutrition: Cal 306; Fat 3 g; Carb 15 g; Protein 4 g
Serving 1; Cook time 10 min

Ingredients
- 1 cup plain unsweetened almond milk
- 4 cups loosely packed spinach that's about 2 large handfuls
- 1 medium avocado peeled and pitted banana
- cup pineapple (frozen)
- 1 cup strawberries (frozen)
- 1 serving Protein Smoothie Boost

Instructions
1. Place all of the ingredients in your blender, and blend until you get a creamy smoothie.

ALKALINE VEGETABLES SMOOTHIE CUBES

Nutrition: Cal 28; Fat 3 g; Carb 6 g; Protein 4 g
Serving 1; Cook time 10 min

Ingredients
- 3/4 cup lime (juice)
- 1 cucumber (peeled if desired, cut into chunks)
- 1 cup kale (tough stems removed, chopped)
- 1 cup collard greens (tough stems removed, chopped)
- 1/2 cup fresh parsley (leaves and tender stems)
- alkaline water (for blending)

Instructions
1. Place all of the ingredients in your blender, and blend until you get a creamy smoothie.

PINEAPPLE GINGER SMOOTHIE

Nutrition: Cal 263; Fat 3 g; Carb 46 g; Protein 4 g
Serving 1; Cook time 10 min

Ingredients
- 1 cup kale (baby)
- 1 orange (peeled)
- 1 inch ginger root
- 1 cup almond milk
- 1/2 cup pineapple (frozen)
- 1/2 cup strawberries (frozen)
- 1 tablespoon chia seeds

Instructions
1. Place all of the ingredients in your blender, and blend until you get a creamy smoothie.

ISLAND GREEN SMOOTHIE

Nutrition: Cal 235; Fat 3 g; Carb 58 g; Protein 4 g
Serving 1; Cook time 10 min

Ingredients
- 1 cup spinach
- 1/2 cup coconut water (unsweetened)
- 1 orange (peeled)
- 1/2 cup pineapple
- 1/2 cup mango
- 1/2 banana

Instructions
1. Place all of the ingredients in your blender, and blend until you get a creamy smoothie.

KALE RECHARGE SMOOTHIE

Nutrition: Cal 58; Fat 0 g; Carb 52 g; Protein 4 g
Serving 1; Cook time 10 min

Ingredients
- 1 frozen, very ripe banana
- 1 Tbsp fresh parsley (or cilantro)
- 3/4 cup spinach, loosely packed
- 1 tsp ginger, grated
- 3/4 cups curly kale, stems removed, loosely packed
- 1/2 cup carrots, chopped

- 1 tsp lime juice
- 8 ounces water
- 4 ice cubes

Instructions
1. Place all of the ingredients in your blender, and blend until you get a creamy smoothie.

SPRIG OF PARSLEY

Nutrition: Cal 214; Fat 3 g; Carb 22 g; Protein 4 g
Serving 1; Cook time 10 min

Ingredients
- 1/4 cup fresh parsley (include the stems)
- 1/2 cup watercress
- 1/2 cup frozen strawberries
- 1/2 frozen banana
- 1 teaspoon chia seeds
- 1 scoop plain plant-based protein powder
- Water to blend (optional)

Instructions
1. Place all of the ingredients in your blender, and blend until you get a creamy smoothie.

GREEN CINNAMON SMOOTHIE

Nutrition: Cal 309; Fat 3 g; Carb 55g; Protein 4 g
Serving 1; Cook time 10 min

Ingredients
- 3 Tbsp rolled oats
- 2 Tbsp sliced almonds or 1 Tbsp almond butter
- medium ripe banana
- 1/4 frozen raspberries or blueberries
- 2 large or 6 small frozen strawberries
- 1/2 cup cold water
- 2 1/2 cups packed fresh spinach
- 6 ice cubes
- 1/4 tsp cinnamon + 1/8 tsp vanilla extract - for blueberry version
- 1/8 tsp almond extract - for raspberry version

Instructions
1. Place all of the ingredients in your blender, and blend until you get a creamy smoothie.

STRAWBERRY SPINACH GREEN SMOOTHIE

Nutrition: Cal 142; Fat 3 g; Carb 28 g; Protein 4 g
Serving 1; Cook time 10 min

Ingredients
- 1/2 very ripe bananas, peeled, diced and frozen
- 6 oz fresh strawberries, hulled (about 9 medium)
- 2 mandarin oranges, peeled and halved
- 3 cups packed baby spinach*
- cup cold water
- 1 cup ice

Instructions
1. Place all of the ingredients in your blender, and blend until you get a creamy smoothie.

MANGO GREEN TEA SMOOTHIE

Nutrition: Cal 126; Fat 0 g; Carb 31 g; Protein 4 g
Serving 1; Cook time 10 min

Ingredients
- 1/2 cups brewed and fully chilled green tea (it works best to prepare it the night before, refrigerate, then remove tea packets the following morning)
- 1/2 cups (8.5 oz) frozen diced mangos
- medium ripe bananas
- cups (2.5 oz) packed fresh spinach
- 1 Tbsp fresh lemon juice
- 1 small handful fresh mint (optional, I like it with or without)

Instructions
1. Place all of the ingredients in your blender, and blend until you get a creamy smoothie.

COLD BUSTER GREEN SMOOTHIE

Nutrition: Cal 259; Fat 3 g; Carb 51 g; Protein 4 g
Serving 1; Cook time 10 min

Ingredients
- cup plain Kefir
- 1/2 cup cold water
- 1/2 Tbsp fresh lemon juice
- 1 cup packed (30g) baby kale
- 1/2 cups (slightly heaping) frozen pineapple chunks
- 1 ripe kiwis, peeled
- 1/4 tsp turmeric
- 1 tsp ginger paste or minced ginger
- 1/2 Tbsp honey

Instructions
1. Place all of the ingredients in your blender, and blend until you get a creamy smoothie.

AVOCADO GREEN SMOOTHIE

Nutrition: Cal 230; Fat 3 g; Carb 34 g; Protein 4 g
Serving 1; Cook time 10 min

Ingredients
- 1 medium avocado
- 1 large granny smith apple , chilled, cored and sliced
- 1 ripe banana , peeled and frozen (use one with spots)
- 1 Navel orange , chilled and peeled
- 2 cups (76g) packed spinach
- 1 cup almond milk , chilled*
- Juice of 1 lime
- tsp honey , or to taste (optional)
- 8 ice cubes (about 1 1/3 cups)

Instructions
1. Place all of the ingredients in your blender, and blend until you get a creamy smoothie.

KALE AND KIWI GREEN SMOOTHIE

Nutrition: Cal 210; Fat 3 g; Carb 46 g; Protein 4 g
Serving 1; Cook time 10 min

Ingredients
- 2 cups packed kale leaves

- 2 ripe bananas, sliced and frozen
- 1/2 cups unsweetened almond milk
- 3 ripe kiwis, peeled and quartered
- 1 tablespoon maple syrup, or to taste

Instructions
1. Place all of the ingredients in your blender, and blend until you get a creamy smoothie.

AVOCOLADA SMOOTHIE

Nutrition: Cal 204; Fat 3 g; Carb 31 g; Protein 4 g
Serving 1; Cook time 10 min

Ingredients
- 1/2 avocado, peeled and pitted
- 1/2 cups frozen pineapple
- 1 cup spinach
- 1 cup coconut water
- teaspoons honey or maple syrup

Instructions
1. Place all of the ingredients in your blender, and blend until you get a creamy smoothie.

MAGIC BROCCOLI SMOOTHIE

Nutrition: Cal 302; Fat 3 g; Carb 60 g; Protein 4 g
Serving 1; Cook time 10 min

Ingredients
- 1/2 cup Greek yogurt
- 1/2 cup water
- 1 cup chopped small broccoli florets
- 1 large green apple, chopped
- 1 banana (room temperature)
- 1 cup frozen pineapple chunks

Instructions
1. Place all of the ingredients in your blender, and blend until you get a creamy smoothie.

BEST KALE SMOOTHIE

Nutrition: Cal 318; Fat 3 g; Carb 81 g; Protein 4 g
Serving 1; Cook time 10 min

Ingredients
- 1 large green apple
- 1 banana
- cups baby kale leaves, loosely packed (or Tuscan or curly kale, roughly chopped)
- 1/2 cup water
- 10 ice cubes
- 0.5 cups frozen pineapple or mango
- 1 tablespoon fresh squeezed lemon juice

Instructions
1. Place all of the ingredients in your blender, and blend until you get a creamy smoothie.

PERFECT CELERY SMOOTHIE

Nutrition: Cal 130; Fat 3 g; Carb 30 g; Protein 4 g
Serving 1; Cook time 10 min

Ingredients
- 4 medium ribs celery (¾ cup chopped)
- 1 large green apple
- 1 banana
- ½ teaspoon peeled and grated ginger (from fresh ginger root)
- 2 cups baby spinach leaves
- ½ cup water
- 10 ice cubes
- 1 ½ tablespoons fresh squeezed lemon juice (1/2 lemon)

Instructions
1. Place all of the ingredients in your blender, and blend until you get a creamy smoothie.

EASY CUCUMBER SMOOTHIE

Nutrition: Cal 174; Fat 1 g; Carb 29 g; Protein 4 g
Serving 1; Cook time 10 min

Ingredients
- 1/2 cup Greek yogurt (or coconut milk)
- cup peeled* and chopped cucumber (standard or English cucumber)
- 1 ripe banana, broken into pieces
- 1 cup frozen pineapple
- 1 handful spinach leaves
- 10 ice cubes
- 1 tablespoon lime juice or lemon juice

Instructions
1. Place all of the ingredients in your blender, and blend until you get a creamy smoothie.

GLOWING GREEN SMOOTHIE

Nutrition: Cal 196; Fat 3 g; Carb 28 g; Protein 4 g
Serving 1; Cook time 10 min

Ingredients
- 1 large green apple
- 1 tablespoon maple syrup
- 1/2 cup water
- 1/4 cup raw cashews
- 2 cups spinach
- 10 ice cubes
- 1 tablespoon fresh squeezed lemon juice

Instructions
1. Place all of the ingredients in your blender, and blend until you get a creamy smoothie.

PERFECT AVOCADO SMOOTHIE

Nutrition: Cal 305; Fat 1 g; Carb 58 g; Protein 4 g
Serving 1; Cook time 10 min

Ingredients
- 1/2 ripe avocado
- 1 large green apple
- 1 banana
- 1 cup baby spinach or kale, loosely packed (or other chopped greens)
- 1/2 cup water
- 1 cup frozen pineapple chunks
- 10 ice cubes
- 1 tablespoon lemon juice

Instructions
1. Place all of the ingredients in your blender, and blend until you get a creamy smoothie.

BEST SPINACH SMOOTHIE

Nutrition: Cal 170; Fat 3 g; Carb 21 g; Protein 4 g
Serving 1; Cook time 10 min

Ingredients
- 1 large green apple
- 1/2 cup water
- 1/4 cup raw cashews (or 1 banana and 1 ½ cups frozen mango or pineapple, skip the maple)
- 4 cups baby spinach leaves or chopped spinach, loosely packed

Instructions
1. Place all of the ingredients in your blender, and blend until you get a creamy smoothie.

GLOWING GREEN BANAN SMOOTHIE

Nutrition: Cal 350; Fat 3 g; Carb 82 g; Protein 4 g
Serving 1; Cook time 10 min

Ingredients
- 1-2 frozen bananas
- 1/2 cup frozen mango
- 1 cup fresh spinach
- splash of almond milk

Instructions
1. Place all of the ingredients in your blender, and blend until you get a creamy smoothie.

CREAMY GREEN SMOOTHIE

Nutrition: Cal 236; Fat 3 g; Carb 23 g; Protein 4 g
Serving 1; Cook time 10 min

Ingredients
- 1/2 cup almond milk
- 1/4 cup spinach
- scoop vanilla protein powder
- 1/4 cup green grapes
- 1/4 cup vanilla Greek yogurt
- 1/4 avocado

Instructions
1. Place all of the ingredients in your blender, and blend until you get a creamy smoothie.

GREEN BREAKFAST SMOOTHIE

Nutrition: Cal 243; Fat 3 g; Carb 27 g; Protein 4 g
Serving 1; Cook time 10 min

Ingredients
- handful spinach (about 50g/2oz), roughly chopped
- 1/2 broccoli florets, roughly chopped
- celery sticks
- tbsp desiccated coconut
- 1 banana
- 1 cup rice milk
- 1/4 tsp spirulina or 1 scoop of greens powder or vegan protein powder (optional)

Instructions
1. Place all of the ingredients in your blender, and blend until you get a creamy smoothie.

PINEAPPLE AVOCADO GREEN SMOOTHIE

Nutrition: Cal 397; Fat 3 g; Carb 41 g; Protein 4 g
Serving 1; Cook time 10 min

Ingredients
- 1/2 cup lite unsweetened coconut milk
- cup packed spinach (35 grams)
- 1/2 heaping cup frozen pineapple (70 grams)
- 1/2 small green apple, roughly chopped (100 grams)
- 1/2 small avocado (50 grams)
- 1 tablespoon chia seeds
- 1 tablespoon lime juice
- 1/2-1 inch fresh ginger
- 1-2 scoops vanilla protein powder or collagen (optional)

Instructions
1. Place all of the ingredients in your blender, and blend until you get a creamy smoothie.

BANANA MATCHA SMOOTHIE

Nutrition: Cal 203; Fat 3 g; Carb 39 g; Protein 4 g
Serving 1; Cook time 10 min

Ingredients
- cup banana slices, frozen
- 1 teaspoon matcha powder
- 1 cup fresh spinach, packed
- 2 teaspoons flax seed
- 1 teaspoon vanilla extract
- 3/4 cup unsweetened almond milk

Instructions
1. Place all of the ingredients in your blender, and blend until you get a creamy smoothie.

MANGO MATCHA GREEN TEA SMOOTHIE

Nutrition: Cal 360; Fat 7 g; Carb 70g; Protein 4 g
Serving 1; Cook time 10 min

Ingredients
- 2 cups fresh spinach
- ½ cups frozen mango chunks
- 1 large frozen banana cut into chunks
- 1 cup frozen broccoli florets
- tablespoon chia seeds
- 1 teaspoon matcha powder
- 2 cups oat milk or other plant based milk
- 1 medium lime juiced

Instructions
1. Place all of the ingredients in your blender, and blend until you get a creamy smoothie.

IRON RICH TROPICAL GREEN SMOOTHIE

Nutrition: Cal 271; Fat 3 g; Carb 62 g; Protein 4 g
Serving 1; Cook time 10 min

Ingredients
- 2 cups baby spinach washed
- 2 cups kale washed, stems removed
- 1 mandarin orange peeled
- 1 lemon juiced
- 1 cup pineapple fresh or frozen
- 1/2 cup orange juice
- 8 ounces iced water

Instructions
1. Place all of the ingredients in your blender, and blend until you get a creamy smoothie.

HEALTHY MANGO SPINACH SMOOTHIE

Nutrition: Cal 292; Fat 3 g; Carb 68 g; Protein 4 g
Serving 1; Cook time 10 min

Ingredients
- cup mango frozen mango chunks or fresh mango
- 1 banana peeled, fresh or frozen
- cups baby spinach about 3 large hand fulls
- 1/2 cup oat milk almond milk, soy milk, coconut milk, or dairy milk can be used.
- 1/2 cup ice cubes
- 1/2 cup water
- 1/2 lemon juiced

Instructions
1. Place all of the ingredients in your blender, and blend until you get a creamy smoothie.

REFRESHING KALE APPLE SMOOTHIE

Nutrition: Cal 197; Fat 3 g; Carb 50 g; Protein 4 g
Serving 1; Cook time 10 min

Ingredients
- 2 cups kale washed, stems removed
- lemon juiced
- Medjool Dates pitted
- Fuji Apples cored with peelings on
- 8 ounces iced water

Instructions
1. Place all of the ingredients in your blender, and blend until you get a creamy smoothie.

TROPICAL MATCHA SMOOTHIE

Nutrition: Cal 191; Fat 3 g; Carb 33 g; Protein 4 g
Serving 1; Cook time 10 min

Ingredients
- 2 cups spinach
- cup mango
- 1 cup almond milk
- 1/2 cup water
- pitted dates
- 1 tablespoon hemp seeds, optional
- 1 teaspoon matcha green tea powder
- 1/2 inch fresh ginger

Instructions
1. Place all of the ingredients in your blender, and blend until you get a creamy smoothie.

MORNING GREEN SMOOTHIE

Nutrition: Cal 204; Fat 3 g; Carb 39 g; Protein 4 g
Serving 1; Cook time 10 min

Ingredients
- 2 cups spinach
- 1 banana, sliced
- 1 cup almond milk
- 1/2 cup water
- 1/4 lime, juiced
- 2 tablespoons chia seeds
- 2 Medjool dates, optional, for added sweetness

Instructions
1. Place all of the ingredients in your blender, and blend until you get a creamy smoothie.

KALE PINEAPPLE SMOOTHIE

Nutrition: Cal 205; Fat 3 g; Carb 38 g; Protein 4 g
Serving 1; Cook time 10 min

Ingredients
- 2 cups kale
- 2 cups unsweetened almond milk
- cup pineapple
- 1 tablespoon chia seeds
- Medjool dates
- 1 cup ice

Instructions
1. Place all of the ingredients in your blender, and blend until you get a creamy smoothie.

PISTACHIO SMOOTHIE

Nutrition: Cal 469; Fat 3 g; Carb 31 g; Protein 4 g
Serving 1; Cook time 10 min

Ingredients
- 1/3 cup pistachios shelled
- 1/2 cup spinach or other leafy vegetable (e.g. lettuce)
- 1/2 cup green apple or 1/2 – 1 apple peeled and cored
- 1/2 avocado
- 1 teaspoon lemon or lime
- 1 cup almond milk or other type of milk (dairy or non-dairy)
- 1/2 teaspoon vanilla extract or almond extract
- tiny pinch fine salt
- 1/2 cup ice optional (or add more milk if not using)

Instructions
1. Place all of the ingredients in your blender, and blend until you get a creamy smoothie.

FROZEN SPINACH SMOOTHIE WITH GINGER ROOT

Nutrition: Cal 147; Fat 3 g; Carb 27g; Protein 4 g
Serving 1; Cook time 10 min

Ingredients
- ½ cup frozen spinach
- 1 ripe pear
- 1 inch fresh ginger knob or 1 teaspoon ground ginger (2.5 cm)
- 1 cup almond milk
- 1 tablespoon maple syrup or one pitted date
- 1 teaspoon chia seeds or flax meal
- 1/8 pumpkin spice mix or cinnamon

Optional
- 1 tablespoon Organic Protein Plant-Based Powder
- 1-2 teaspoons maca powder

Instructions
1. Place all of the ingredients in your blender, and blend until you get a creamy smoothie.

PINEAPPLE AND CUCUMBER SMOOTHIE FOR WEIGHT LOSS

Nutrition: Cal 138; Fat 3 g; Carb 32 g; Protein 4 g
Serving 1; Cook time 10 min

Ingredients
- 1 cup sliced cucumber skins on
- ½ cup frozen pineapple if using fresh, add 4-6 ice cubes
- 1 ripe pear cored
- ½ cup almond milk or light coconut milk
- ½ cup iced water or with 4 ice cubes
- ½ medium lemon juiced (~1 Tablespoon (15 ml) juice per ½ lemon)
- slices fresh ginger peeled, or ½ teaspoon ginger powder

Optional
- cup spinach for a green smoothie
- teaspoons maca powder for enhanced energy and stamina

Instructions
1. Place all of the ingredients in your blender, and blend until you get a creamy smoothie.

AVOCOLADA KALE TROPICAL SMOOTHIE

Nutrition: Cal 316; Fat 3 g; Carb 40 g; Protein 4 g
Serving 1; Cook time 10 min

Ingredients
- cup avocado cut into chunks
- 1 1/2 cups pineapple frozen
- 1/2 cup spinach
- 1/2 cup kale
- 1 tablespoon agave nectar
- 1 tablespoon lime juice
- 1 cup coconut water

Instructions
1. Place all of the ingredients in your blender, and blend until you get a creamy smoothie.

BROCCOLI SMOOTHIE

Nutrition: Cal 138; Fat 3 g; Carb 31 g; Protein 4 g
Serving 1; Cook time 10 min

Ingredients
- 1/2 cup broccoli
- cup frozen pineapple
- 1 cup honeydew melon
- 1/2 cup vegan yogurt
- 2 teaspoons maple syrup
- 1/2 cup spinach

Instructions
1. Place all of the ingredients in your blender, and blend until you get a creamy smoothie.

GREEN CHIA SMOOTHIE

Nutrition: Cal 142; Fat 3 g; Carb 31 g; Protein 4 g
Serving 1; Cook time 10 min

Ingredients
- kale 2 handfuls
- spinach 2 handfuls
- pineapple ¼ pcs.
- mango 1 pc.
- banana 1 pc.
- lemon 1 pc.
- water 100 ml
- chia seeds 2 tsp

Instructions
1. Place all of the ingredients in your blender, and blend until you get a creamy smoothie.

GLOWING GREEN CHIA SMOOTHIE

Nutrition: Cal 134; Fat 3 g; Carb 30 g; Protein 4 g
Serving 1; Cook time 10 min

Ingredients
- cup raw coconut water or filtered water
- 1 cup firmly packed baby spinach
- 1 English cucumber, roughly chopped (do not peel)
- cups diced ripe fresh pineapple
- 1 ½ tsp. finely grated lime zest, plus more to taste
- Tbs. fresh lime juice, plus more to taste
- 1/8 tsp. ground turmeric

Instructions
1. Place all of the ingredients in your blender, and blend until you get a creamy smoothie.

CREAMY GREEN CHIA SMOOTHIE

Nutrition: Cal 366; Fat 3 g; Carb 42 g; Protein 4 g
Serving 1; Cook time 10 min

Ingredients
- cup Almond milk
- 1/2 tbsp Chia seeds
- 1 tsp Coconut oil
- 1 scoop (30g) Whey protein powder

- 1 cup Spinach
- 1 medium Banana
- 1/2 tsp Vanilla extract

Instructions
1. Place all of the ingredients in your blender, and blend until you get a creamy smoothie.

BASIC GREEN SMOOTHIE

Nutrition: Cal 134; Fat 3 g; Carb 23g; Protein 4 g
Serving 1; Cook time 10 min

Ingredients
- cup Water
- 1 cup Mixed Fruit
- 4 cup Spinach
- 1/4 pinch Cayenne pepper
- 3,5 grams Chia seeds
- 1/2 tbsp, ground Flaxseed

Instructions
1. Place all of the ingredients in your blender, and blend until you get a creamy smoothie.

GREEN MONSTER SMOOTHIE

Nutrition: Cal 293; Fat 3 g; Carb 45 g; Protein 4 g
Serving 1; Cook time 10 min

Ingredients
- 3/4 cup, unthawed trawberries
- 1/2 medium Cucumber
- medium Banana
- 1 cup Spinach
- 1,5 scoops Collagen Peptides
- 1 tbsp Chia seeds
- 1 cup Water

Instructions
1. Place all of the ingredients in your blender, and blend until you get a creamy smoothie.

GREEN KIWI SMOOTHIE

Nutrition: Cal 370; Fat 3 g; Carb 89 g; Protein 4 g
Serving 1; Cook time 10 min

Ingredients
- cucumber (8-1/4") Cucumber
- 1 extra large (9" or longer) Banana
- 4 fruit (2" dia) Kiwi fruit
- cup Spinach

Instructions
1. Place all of the ingredients in your blender, and blend until you get a creamy smoothie.

KALE & PINEAPPLE SMOOTHIE

Nutrition: Cal 213; Fat 3 g; Carb 41 g; Protein 4 g
Serving 1; Cook time 10 min

Ingredients
- 1 cup baby kale
- 1/4 cup plain or coconut Greek yogurt
- 1 cup frozen pineapple chunks
- 1/2 cup unsweetened vanilla coconut milk
- 1/2 cup fresh orange juice

Instructions
1. Place all of the ingredients in your blender, and blend until you get a creamy smoothie.

BRAIN FOOD SMOOTHIE

Nutrition: Cal 392; Fat 3 g; Carb 56 g; Protein 4 g
Serving 1; Cook time 10 min

Ingredients
- 1/2 cups spinach
- cup coconut water
- 1 pear (ripe + cored)
- 1/2 cup mango (frozen)
- 1/4 avocado
- tablespoon hemp hearts

Instructions
1. Place all of the ingredients in your blender, and blend until you get a creamy smoothie.

ROMAINE AROUND SMOOTHIE

Nutrition: Cal 280; Fat 3 g; Carb 27 g; Protein 4 g
Serving 1; Cook time 10 min

Ingredients
- 1 cup romaine lettuce
- 1/2 cup spinach
- 1/2 apple with peel, seeded and quartered
- 1 tablespoon chia seeds
- 1/2 cup unsweetened almond milk
- 1 scoop plain plant-based protein powder
- Water to blend

Instructions
1. Place all of the ingredients in your blender, and blend until you get a creamy smoothie.

TEA FOR ONE SMOOTHIE

Nutrition: Cal 245; Fat 3 g; Carb 23 g; Protein 4 g
Serving 1; Cook time 10 min

Ingredients
- cup green tea
- 1/2 frozen banana
- 1,5 tablespoons fresh lemon juice
- 1/8 avocado
- 1 scoop vanilla plant-based protein powder
- Water to blend (optional)

Instructions
1. Place all of the ingredients in your blender, and blend until you get a creamy smoothie.

BEST GREEN SMOOTHIE

Nutrition: Cal 209; Fat 3 g; Carb 34 g; Protein 4 g
Serving 1; Cook time 10 min

Ingredients
- ½ cups unsweetened almond milk
- 2 cups spinach* frozen
- 1 medium banana frozen
- 1 cup fruit of choice

Instructions
1. Place all of the ingredients in your blender, and blend until you get a creamy smoothie.

HOW TO MAKE A SMOOTHIE

Nutrition: Cal 153; Fat 3 g; Carb 33 g; Protein 4 g
Serving 1; Cook time 10 min

Ingredients
- ½ cups unsweetened almond milk
- 1 cup greens, frozen
- 1 medium banana, frozen
- 1 cup fruit, frozen
- TBS add-ins (protein powder, collagen, honey, etc).

Instructions
1. Place all of the ingredients in your blender, and blend until you get a creamy smoothie.

AVOCADO APPLE GREEN SMOOTHIE

Nutrition: Cal 163; Fat 3 g; Carb 29 g; Protein 4 g
Serving 1; Cook time 10 min

Ingredients
- 1/2 cup nut milk, or dairy milk
- 2 cups spinach
- 1 frozen banana
- 1 apple
- 1/4 avocado
- plus optional add-ins

Instructions
1. Place all of the ingredients in your blender, and blend until you get a creamy smoothie.

SCRUB YOURSELF CLEAN GREEN SMOOTHIE

Nutrition: Cal 156; Fat 3 g; Carb 30 g; Protein 4 g
Serving 1; Cook time 10 min

Ingredients
- ½ cup strawberries
- ¼ cup pineapple
- 1 cup broccoli florets
- 1 teaspoon honey
- 1 cup almond milk

Instructions
1. Place all of the ingredients in your blender, and blend until you get a creamy smoothie.

METABOLISM BOOSTING GREEN SMOOTHIE

Nutrition: Cal 144; Fat 3 g; Carb 28 g; Protein 4 g
Serving 1; Cook time 10 min

Ingredients
- 1 orange peeled
- ⅓ cup strawberries
- 1 cup raw spinach
- 1 cup almond milk

Instructions
1. Place all of the ingredients in your blender, and blend until you get a creamy smoothie.

STRAWBERRY BANANA GREEN SMOOTHIE

Nutrition: Cal 207; Fat 3 g; Carb 42 g; Protein 4 g
Serving 1; Cook time 10 min

Ingredients
- ½ cup strawberries
- 1 banana
- 1 cup raw spinach
- ½ cup almond milk
- 1 teaspoon vanilla extract

Instructions
1. Place all of the ingredients in your blender, and blend until you get a creamy smoothie.

APPLE PIE GREEN SMOOTHIE

Nutrition: Cal 165; Fat 3 g; Carb 34 g; Protein 4 g
Serving 1; Cook time 10 min

Ingredients
- apple peeled and cored
- ¼ cup blueberries
- ¼ teaspoon cinnamon
- ⅛ teaspoon nutmeg
- 1 cup spinach
- 1 tablespoon chia seeds
- 1 teaspoon vanilla extract
- 1 cup water

Instructions
1. Place all of the ingredients in your blender, and blend until you get a creamy smoothie.

ELECTRIC GREEN BOOST SMOOTHIE

Nutrition: Cal 174; Fat 3 g; Carb 36 g; Protein 4 g
Serving 1; Cook time 10 min

Ingredients
- ¼ cup pineapple
- orange peeled
- 1 cup raw spinach
- 1 cup almond milk

Instructions
1. Place all of the ingredients in your blender, and blend until you get a creamy smoothie.

CRISP MANGO CUCUMBER GREEN SMOOTHIE

Nutrition: Cal 153; Fat 3 g; Carb 30 g; Protein 42g
Serving 1; Cook time 10 min

Ingredients
- ¼ cup mango
- orange peeled
- 1 cup chopped cucumber
- 1 tablespoon flax seeds
- 1 cup spinach

Instructions
1. Place all of the ingredients in your blender, and blend until you get a creamy smoothie.

GREEN TROPICAL SUNRISE

Nutrition: Cal 176; Fat 3 g; Carb 36 g; Protein 4 g
Serving 1; Cook time 10 min

Ingredients
- ¼ cup pineapple
- orange peeled
- 1 carrot
- 1 cup spinach
- 1 tablespoon flax seeds
- 1 cup water

Instructions
1. Place all of the ingredients in your blender, and blend until you get a creamy smoothie.

CRAZY FOR KALE

Nutrition: Cal 222; Fat 3 g; Carb 48 g; Protein 4 g
Serving 1; Cook time 10 min

Ingredients
- ½ cup cherries
- ½ cup blueberries
- cup fresh kale
- teaspoons honey
- 1 cup almond milk

Instructions
1. Place all of the ingredients in your blender, and blend until you get a creamy smoothie.

TROPICAL GREEN COCONUT MILK SMOOTHIE

Nutrition: Cal 157; Fat 3 g; Carb 35 g; Protein 4 g
Serving 1; Cook time 10 min

Ingredients
- cup baby spinach
- 1 banana sliced and frozen
- 1/4 cup frozen mango chunks
- 1/2 cup unsweetened coconut milk
- 1/2 cup ice
- scoops Vanilla Protein Powder optional

Instructions
1. Place all of the ingredients in your blender, and blend until you get a creamy smoothie.

RASPBERRY-BANANA GREEN SMOOTHIE

Nutrition: Cal 164; Fat 3 g; Carb 36 g; Protein 4 g
Serving 1; Cook time 10 min

Ingredients
- ½ cup raspberries
- 1 banana
- 1 cup raw baby spinach
- ½ cup unsweetened almond milk

Instructions
1. Place all of the ingredients in your blender, and blend until you get a creamy smoothie.

WEIGHT LOSS GREEN SMOOTHIE

Nutrition: Cal 211; Fat 3 g; Carb 41 g; Protein 4 g
Serving 1; Cook time 10 min

Ingredients
- 2 cups baby spinach
- 1 cup blueberries frozen
- 1 banana sliced and frozen
- 1/2 cup unsweetened almond milk
- 1 kiwi peeled and quartered
- 1 scoop vanilla protein powder (optional)
- 1/2 cup Greek Yogurt

Instructions
1. Place all of the ingredients in your blender, and blend until you get a creamy smoothie.

CHIA BERRY GREEN PROTEIN SMOOTHIE

Nutrition: Cal 255; Fat 3 g; Carb 32 g; Protein 4 g
Serving 1; Cook time 10 min

Ingredients
- 1 cup water
- 1 cup Spinach
- 1/2 cup Frozen berries
- 1/2 medium Banana frozen
- 1 tbsp Chia seeds

Instructions
1. Place all of the ingredients in your blender, and blend until you get a creamy smoothie.

FOOD PROCESSOR SMOOTHIE

Nutrition: Cal 215; Fat 3 g; Carb 23 g; Protein 4 g
Serving 1; Cook time 10 min

Ingredients
- 3 handfuls baby spinach
- 1/2 cups frozen mango chunks
- 1/2 cup frozen pineapple niblets
- tablespoons nut butter (I like almond butter or peanut butter)
- 1 1/2 cups unsweetened plant milk (I like almond milk)
- 1–2 scoops protein powder (optional, for added nutrition)

Instructions
1. Place all of the ingredients in your blender, and blend until you get a creamy smoothie.

SPIRULINA SMOOTHIE

Nutrition: Cal 407; Fat 3 g; Carb 56 g; Protein 4 g
Serving 1; Cook time 10 min

Ingredients
- large Frozen Banana - peeled, cut in chunks, and frozen the day before
- ½ cup Frozen Mango - or frozen pineapple
- ½ Ripe Avocado - cored
- ½ cup Baby Spinach - 0.7 oz
- 1 1 ¼ cup Almond Milk - or plant-based milk of choice
- 1 teaspoon Spirulina Powder - green spirulina or use blue spirulina for a neutral, no fishy flavor
- 1 tablespoon Hemp Seeds - or chia seeds
- 1-2 teaspoons Maple Syrup - or a pinch of stevia powder
- ¼ teaspoon Vanilla Extract

Instructions
1. Place all of the ingredients in your blender, and blend until you get a creamy smoothie.

IRON RICH SMOOTHIE

Nutrition: Cal 267; Fat 3 g; Carb 53 g; Protein 4 g
Serving 1; Cook time 10 min

Ingredients
- 1 cup orange juice
- 1 ripe kiwi, cut in half (peeled or unpeeled)
- 1 frozen banana, broken into chunks
- 1 pitted date or prune
- handfuls baby spinach
- 2 tablespoons unsalted raw pumpkin seeds
- 2 tablespoons cacao powder or cocoa powder
- 1 tablespoon blackstrap molasses

Instructions
1. Place all of the ingredients in your blender, and blend until you get a creamy smoothie.

GREEN APPLE SMOOTHIE

Nutrition: Cal 233; Fat 3 g; Carb 44 g; Protein 4 g
Serving 1; Cook time 10 min

Ingredients
- cup unsweetened almond milk (or your choice of milk)
- 1/2 cup vanilla yogurt (use plant-based yogurt for dairy-free diets)
- 1 green apple, cored and cut into quarters
- 1 frozen ripe banana, broken in half
- 1/2 cup frozen pineapple niblets or frozen chunks
- 1 tablespoon chia seeds or flax seeds
- 1 handful baby spinach
- 1/2 cup ice cubes

Instructions
1. Place all of the ingredients in your blender, and blend until you get a creamy smoothie.

BROCCOLI SMOOTHIE WITH PINEAPPLE

Nutrition: Cal 199; Fat 3 g; Carb 31 g; Protein 4 g
Serving 1; Cook time 10 min

Ingredients
- 1/2 cups unsweetened plant milk (I used almond milk)
- cup fresh or frozen broccoli florets
- 1/2 cup fresh frozen pineapple tidbits
- 1/2 cup frozen mango chunks
- 1 frozen banana, broken into chunks
- 1/2 avocado, peeled with the core removed
- 1/2 cup ice cubes (optional, to thicken)

Instructions
1. Place all of the ingredients in your blender, and blend until you get a creamy smoothie.

COLLARD GREENS SMOOTHIE

Nutrition: Cal 142; Fat 3 g; Carb 28 g; Protein 4 g
Serving 1; Cook time 10 min

Ingredients
- large bunch of collard greens
- 1,5 cups carrot juice
- 1/4 cup hemp seeds
- 1 cup frozen sweet cherries or any frozen berry
- 1/2 cup frozen mango chunks
- 1/4 cup frozen pineapple chunks
- 1 tablespoon cocoa or cacao powder

Instructions
1. Place all of the ingredients in your blender, and blend until you get a creamy smoothie.

AWESOME AVOCADO AND BANANA SMOOTHIE

Nutrition: Cal 300; Fat 3 g; Carb 47 g; Protein 40g
Serving 1; Cook time 10 min

Ingredients
- ripe banana, sliced
- 1 avocado, peel and remove stone
- 1,5 teaspoons honey (optional)
- 1/4 teaspoon vanilla extract
- cups low-fat milk, chilled
- 6 ice cubes

Instructions
1. Place all of the ingredients in your blender, and blend until you get a creamy smoothie.

KETO AVOCADO SMOOTHIE

Nutrition: Cal 452; Fat 41g; Carb 21 g; Protein 4 g
Serving 1; Cook time 10 min

Ingredients
- avocado
- 1 tsp vanilla extract
- 1 -2 tbsp monk fruit sweetener
- 1 cup almond milk
- 1 tbsp peanut butter

Instructions

1. Place all of the ingredients in your blender, and blend until you get a creamy smoothie.

FAVORITE GREEN SMOOTHIE

Nutrition: Cal 267; Fat 3 g; Carb 66 g; Protein 4 g
Serving 1; Cook time 10 min

Ingredients
- cup water or milk
- 1/2 cup orange juice (see notes)
- 1 to 2 large handfuls fresh baby spinach
- 1 frozen banana, cut into coins
- 1 cup frozen mango (or other fruit, like frozen strawberries or blueberries)

Instructions
1. Place all of the ingredients in your blender, and blend until you get a creamy smoothie.

ENERGIZING MATCHA SMOOTHIE

Nutrition: Cal 300; Fat 3 g; Carb 58 g; Protein 4 g
Serving 1; Cook time 10 min

Ingredients
- cup water (or almond milk)
- 1 frozen banana
- 1/4 avocado
- 1 cup frozen mango
- 1/2 inch fresh ginger, peeled (optional; add to taste)
- 1 big handful fresh baby spinach
- 1/2 teaspoon matcha powder

Instructions
1. Place all of the ingredients in your blender, and blend until you get a creamy smoothie.

SHAMROCK SMOOTHIE

Nutrition: Cal 412; Fat 3 g; Carb 94 g; Protein 4 g
Serving 1; Cook time 10 min

Ingredients
- 3/4 cup almond milk (or water)
- 1/4 avocado, pitted
- handful fresh baby spinach
- 1/4 teaspoon pure peppermint extract
- 5 Medjool dates, pitted
- 1 to2 large handfuls of ice

Instructions
1. Place all of the ingredients in your blender, and blend until you get a creamy smoothie.

BROCCOLI SPROUT SMOOTHIE

Nutrition: Cal 243; Fat 3 g; Carb 34 g; Protein 4 g
Serving 2 ; Cook time 10 min

Ingredients
- 2 cups filtered water
- 1/4 cup hemp seeds
- 2 cups baby spinach
- 1/2 cup broccoli sprouts, rinsed well
- banana, frozen
- 1 cup frozen strawberries
- 1/4 cup frozen pineapple chunks
- 1 tablespoon cocoa powder

Instructions
1. Place all of the ingredients in your blender, and blend until you get a creamy smoothie.

SPINACH ALMOND SMOOTHIE

Nutrition: Cal 399; Fat 3 g; Carb 34 g; Protein 4 g
Serving 1; Cook time 10 min

Ingredients
- 1/2 cup almond milk, plus more as needed to blend
- 2 cups baby spinach (see notes)
- 1 tablespoon peanut butter (or almond butter)
- 1 tablespoons hemp hearts
- 1 frozen banana, sliced
- 1/4 teaspoon ground cinnamon

Instructions
1. Place all of the ingredients in your blender, and blend until you get a creamy smoothie.

CREAMY ZUCCHINI SMOOTHIE

Nutrition: Cal 342; Fat 3 g; Carb 44 g; Protein 4 g
Serving 1; Cook time 10 min

Ingredients
- 1 cup water
- 1 cup frozen zucchini
- 1 frozen banana, cut into coins
- 1,5 tablespoons peanut butter
- 1 teaspoon honey (or sub 2 pitted Medjool dates)
- 1 handful fresh baby spinach (optional)

Instructions
1. Place all of the ingredients in your blender, and blend until you get a creamy smoothie.

KALE AND GINGER SMOOTHIE

Nutrition: Cal 65.5; Fat 0,4 g; Carb 14 g; Protein 0,7 g
Serving 2; Cook time 10 min

Ingredients
- 2 cups spring water
- 1 cup kale leaves, fresh
- ¼ cup key lime juice
- 1 medium fresh apple, cored
- 1-inch piece of ginger, fresh
- 1 cup sliced cucumber, fresh
- 1 tablespoon of sea moss gel

Instructions
1. Take a high-powered blender, switch it on, and then place all the ingredients inside, in order.
2. Cover the blender with its lid and then pulse at high speed for 1 minute or more until smooth.
3. Distribute the smoothie between two glasses and then serve

SPINACH ALMOND SMOOTHIE

<u>Nutrition: Cal 399; Fat 3 g; Carb 34 g; Protein 4 g</u>
<u>Serving 1; Cook time 10 min</u>

Ingredients
- 1/2 cup almond milk , plus more as needed to blend
- to 2 cups baby spinach (see notes)
- 1 tablespoon peanut butter (or almond butter)
- 1,5 tablespoons hemp hearts
- 1 frozen banana , sliced
- 1/4 teaspoon ground cinnamon

Instructions
1. Place all of the ingredients in your blender, and blend until you get a creamy smoothie.

DANDELION AND WATERCRESS SMOOTHIE

<u>Nutrition: Cal 418; Fat 1,4 g; Carb 96 g; Protein 5,2 g</u>
<u>Serving 1; Cook time 10 min</u>

Ingredients
- 2 cups spring water
- large bunch of dandelion greens, fresh
- ¼ cup key lime juice
- 1 cup of watercress, fresh
- baby bananas, peeled
- ½ cup fresh blueberries
- 1-inch piece of ginger, fresh
- 6 Medjool dates, pitted
- 1 tablespoon burdock root powder

Instructions
1. Place all of the ingredients in your blender, and blend until you get a creamy smoothie.

Smoothie Recipes For Weight Loss

LEAN, MEAN, GREEN MACHINE

Nutrition: Cal 304; Fat 3 g; Carb 47 g; Protein 4 g
Serving 1; Cook time 10 min

Ingredients
- medium banana (cut into pieces)
- 1 kiwi (peeled and cut into pieces)
- 1 cup unsweetened almond milk
- 1 cup spinach
- 1 scoop vanilla whey protein powder
- 1/2 cup coconut water

Instructions
1. Place all of the ingredients in your blender, and blend until you get a creamy smoothie.

BANANA ALMOND PROTEIN SMOOTHIE

Nutrition: Cal 329 Fat 3 g; Carb 26g; Protein 4 g
Serving 1; Cook time 10 min

Ingredients
- ½ cup coconut water
- ½ cup plain Greek yogurt
- 3 tbsp almond butter
- 1 scoop whey protein powder
- 1 tbsp hulled hemp seeds
- 1 frozen banana
- 1 cup ice

Instructions
1. Place all of the ingredients in your blender, and blend until you get a creamy smoothie.

WORKOUT RECOVERY SMOOTHIE

Nutrition: Cal 233; Fat 3 g; Carb 20g; Protein 20g
Serving 1; Cook time 10 min

Ingredients
- ¾ cup ice
- ¼ cup fresh or frozen pitted tart cherries
- ¼ cup pomegranate juice
- 1 scoop vanilla protein powder
- 1 tbsp chopped walnuts
- 1 small cooked, peeled beet (or raw beet, scrubbed and chopped)

Instructions
1. Place all of the ingredients in your blender, and blend until you get a creamy smoothie.

PROTEIN POWER SMOOTHIE

Nutrition: Cal 284; Fat 3 g; Carb 27 g; Protein 4 g
Serving 1; Cook time 10 min

Ingredients
- ¾ cup fat-free milk
- ½ ripe banana
- ½ cup frozen raspberries
- ½ cup frozen blueberries
- scoop vanilla whey protein powder
- 5 ice cubes

Instructions
1. Place all of the ingredients in your blender, and blend until you get a creamy smoothie.

PEACH OAT SMOOTHIE

Nutrition: Cal 142; Fat 3 g; Carb 28 g; Protein 4 g
Serving 1; Cook time 10 min

Ingredients
- 2 ripe peaches
- 1 Tbsp chia seeds
- 1/4 cup rolled oats (gluten-free for GF eaters)
- 1/2 frozen banana (peeled before freezing)
- 1/4 cup fresh orange juice
- 1/2 cup unsweetened almond milk
- 1 Tbsp agave, maple syrup, or a pinch of stevia (*optional /for added sweetness / or honey for non-vegan*

Instructions
1. Place all of the ingredients in your blender, and blend until you get a creamy smoothie.

DOUBLE CHOCOLATE MINT SMOOTHIE

Nutrition: Cal 292; Fat 3 g; Carb 28 g; Protein 25 g
Serving 1; Cook time 10 min

Ingredients
- scoop chocolate protein powder
- 3/4 cup chocolate almond milk
- 1 tbsp walnuts
- tbsp cocoa powder, unsweetened
- 1 tbsp cacao nibs
- mint leaves
- ice cubes
- ¼ cup water

Instructions
1. Place all of the ingredients in your blender, and blend until you get a creamy smoothie.

COCONUT ALMOND SMOOTHIE

Nutrition: Cal 405; Fat 3 g; Carb 33 ; Protein 27 g
Serving 1; Cook time 10 min

Ingredients
- scoop chocolate protein powder
- 1 tbsp unsweetened coconut flakes
- 1 cup chocolate almond milk
- 1 rounded tbsp almond butter
- 1½ cups water
- ice cubes

Instructions
1. Place all of the ingredients in your blender, and blend until you get a creamy smoothie.

BLUEBERRY BREAKFAST SMOOTHIE

Nutrition: Cal 536; Fat 3 g; Carb 42 g; Protein 4 g
Serving 1; Cook time 10 min

Ingredients

- 2 ripe peaches
- 1 cup blueberries
- 1/2 banana
- 1 1/2 scoops protein powder
- 2 tbsp walnuts
- 2 tbsp oats
- 1 tbsp chia seeds

Instructions
1. Place all of the ingredients in your blender, and blend until you get a creamy smoothie.

BERRY-COCONUT SMOOTHIE

Nutrition: Cal 322 Fat 3 g; Carb 28 g; Protein 11 g
Serving 1; Cook time 10 min

Ingredients
- ½ cup cooked red lentils cooled
- ¾ cup unsweetened vanilla coconut milk beverage
- ½ cup frozen mixed berries
- ½ cup frozen sliced banana
- tablespoon unsweetened shredded coconut, plus more for garnish
- 1 teaspoon honey
- ice cubes

Instructions
1. Place all of the ingredients in your blender, and blend until you get a creamy smoothie.

MATCHA MADNESS SMOOTHIE

Nutrition: Cal 412 Fat 3 g; Carb 30 g; Protein 4 g
Serving 1; Cook time 10 min

Ingredients
- 1 cup coconut milk beverage (not canned coconut milk)
- 2 scoops plain or vanilla protein powder
- 1 tsp matcha tea powder
- 1 tbsp cashew butter
- 1 tbsp fresh lime juice
- 1/4 tsp ginger powder
- 1 cup frozen mango cubes

Instructions
1. Place all of the ingredients in your blender, and blend until you get a creamy smoothie.

BLUE BOMB SMOOTHIE

Nutrition: Cal 395 Fat 11 g; Carb 42g; Protein 34 g
Serving 1; Cook time 10 min

Ingredients
- 1 cup milk
- 3/4 cup plain cottage cheese
- 1 tbsp ground flaxseed
- 1 tsp orange zest
- 1 tsp honey
- 1/8 tsp almond extract
- 3/4 cup frozen blueberries

Instructions
1. Place all of the ingredients in your blender, and blend until you get a creamy smoothie.

MANGO-ALMOND SMOOTHIE

Nutrition: Cal 457; Fat 3 g; Carb 45 g; Protein 21g
Serving 1; Cook time 10 min

Ingredients
- ½ cup frozen chopped mango
- ½ cup nonfat plain Greek yogurt
- ¼ cup frozen sliced banana
- ¼ cup plain unsweetened almond milk
- 5 tablespoons unsalted almonds, divided
- ⅛ teaspoon ground allspice
- ¼ cup raspberries
- ½ teaspoon honey

Instructions
1. Place all of the ingredients in your blender, and blend until you get a creamy smoothie.

BERRY BLAST PROTEIN SMOOTHIE

Nutrition: Cal 678 Fat 3 g; Carb 67 g; Protein 4 g
Serving 1; Cook time 10 min

Ingredients
- 2 cups frozen mixed berries
- 1 cup Anchor Manuka Honey Greek Style Yoghurt
- 1 cup Anchor Protein+ Milk
- 1 Banana
- Tbsp oats
- 2 scoops vanilla protein powder (optional)

Instructions
1. Place all of the ingredients in your blender, and blend until you get a creamy smoothie.

FRUIT SMOOTHIE

Nutrition: Cal 186 Fat 3 g; Carb 46 g; Protein 4 g
Serving 1; Cook time 10 min

Ingredients
- cup spinach
- 1 orange (peeled)
- ½ cup strawberries (frozen)
- ½ cup blueberries (frozen)
- ½ banana

Instructions
1. Place all of the ingredients in your blender, and blend until you get a creamy smoothie.

VANILLA MATCHA SMOOTHIE

Nutrition: Cal 270; Fat 3 g; Carb 37g; Protein 4 g
Serving 1; Cook time 10 min

Ingredients
- 2 tablespoon raw cashews
- ¼ cup coconut water
- ¾ cup cashew milk
- teaspoon matcha (or more, if desired)
- 1 banana (frozen)

- 1 teaspoon vanilla extract (optional)
- ¼ teaspoon ginger root (optional)

Instructions
1. Place all of the ingredients in your blender, and blend until you get a creamy smoothie.

GRAPEFRUIT SMOOTHIE

Nutrition: Cal 296 Fat 3 g; Carb 28 g; Protein 5 g
Serving 1; Cook time 10 min

Ingredients
- 1 grapefruit (pink, peeled)
- ½ cup strawberries (frozen)
- 1 banana (peeled)
- 1 cup peach (frozen)

Instructions
1. Place all of the ingredients in your blender, and blend until you get a creamy smoothie.

TROPICAL SMOOTHIE

Nutrition: Cal 180; Fat 3 g; Carb 44 g; Protein 3 g
Serving 1; Cook time 10 min

Ingredients
- 1 orange (peeled)
- ¼ cup water (optional)
- 1 ½ cups strawberries (frozen)
- ½ cup mango (frozen)

Instructions
1. Place all of the ingredients in your blender, and blend until you get a creamy smoothie.

SAVORY TOMATO SMOOTHIE

Nutrition: Cal 83 ; Fat 3 g; Carb 17 g; Protein 4 g
Serving 1; Cook time 10 min

Ingredients
- cup kale (stems removed)
- 1 ½ cups tomato
- ½ stalk celery
- 1 stalk green onions
- ½ clove garlic
- 1 tablespoon lime (juice)
- ⅛ teaspoon cayenne pepper
- pinch sea salt

Instructions
1. Place all of the ingredients in your blender, and blend until you get a creamy smoothie.

EASY FLAXSEED SMOOTHIE

Nutrition: Cal 456; Fat 3 g; Carb 60 g; Protein 4 g
Serving 1; Cook time 10 min

Ingredients
- banana
- 1 cup almond milk
- 1 tablespoon almond butter
- 1 tablespoon ground flaxseed

- 1 medjool date (pitted)
- 1 teaspoon vanilla extract
- ½ teaspoon ground cinnamon

Instructions
1. Place all of the ingredients in your blender, and blend until you get a creamy smoothie.

GRAPEFRUIT SMOOTHIE

Nutrition: Cal 131; Fat 3 g; Carb 33g; Protein 45g
Serving 1; Cook time 10 min

Ingredients
- 1 cup spinach
- ½ cup water
- ½ orange (peeled)
- ½ cup pineapple (frozen)
- ½ banana

Instructions
1. Place all of the ingredients in your blender, and blend until you get a creamy smoothie.

DRAGON FRUIT SMOOTHIE

Nutrition: Cal 146; Fat 3 g; Carb 22 g; Protein 2 g
Serving 1; Cook time 10 min

Ingredients
- ½ cup dragon fruit (frozen cubed)
- ¼ cup mango (frozen)
- ¼ cup pineapple (frozen)
- ¾ cup almond milk
- 1 tablespoon lime (juice)

Instructions
1. Place all of the ingredients in your blender, and blend until you get a creamy smoothie.

HONEY TURMERIC SMOOTHIE

Nutrition: Cal 240; Fat 3 g; Carb 54g; Protein 4 g
Serving 1; Cook time 10 min

Ingredients
- 1 inch ginger root (peeled)
- 1 orange (peeled and zested)
- ¾ cup **almond milk** (or other nut milk)
- ½ cup mango (frozen)
- ½ cup sliced carrots (frozen)
- 1 tablespoon honey
- 1 teaspoon ground turmeric

Instructions
1. Place all of the ingredients in your blender, and blend until you get a creamy smoothie.

PEACH SMOOTHIE

Nutrition: Cal 122; Fat 3 g; Carb 30 g; Protein 4 g
Serving 1; Cook time 10 min

Ingredients
- ½ orange (peeled)
- ½ cup water
- ½ cups peach (frozen)

- 1 teaspoon ginger root (finely minced)

Instructions
1. Place all of the ingredients in your blender, and blend until you get a creamy smoothie.

SUMMER WATERMELON SMOOTHIE

Nutrition: Cal 135; Fat 3 g; Carb 35 g; Protein 4 g
Serving 1; Cook time 10 min

Ingredients
- ¼ cup cherries (frozen)
- 2 cups watermelon (chopped)
- ¼ cup strawberries (frozen)
- ½ lime (peeled)
- tablespoon chia seeds (optional)

Instructions
1. Place all of the ingredients in your blender, and blend until you get a creamy smoothie.

CHERRY ACAÍ SMOOTHIE

Nutrition: Cal 181; Fat 7 g; Carb 29 g; Protein 4 g
Serving 1; Cook time 10 min

Ingredients
- cup cashew milk (unsweetened)
- 1 tablespoon cashews
- ½ banana
- ½ cup cherries (frozen)
- 1 packet açaí puree (frozen)

Instructions
1. Place all of the ingredients in your blender, and blend until you get a creamy smoothie.

PCOS Smoothie

Nutrition: Cal 771; Fat 3 g; Carb 33 g; Protein 10 g
Serving 1; Cook time 10 min

Ingredients
- ½ cup pumpkin puree
- 4 oz carrot (cut into large pieces)
- tablespoon ginger root (minced)
- 1 cup almond milk
- ¾ cup coconut cream
- 1 teaspoon ground cinnamon
- ½ teaspoon ground turmeric
- Pinch black pepper

Instructions
1. Place all of the ingredients in your blender, and blend until you get a creamy smoothie.

PERFECT LEMON SMOOTHIE

Nutrition: Cal 137; Fat 3 g; Carb 35 g; Protein 2 g
Serving 1; Cook time 10 min

Ingredients
- lemon (peeled)
- ½ cup water
- 1 tablespoon honey
- ½ inch ginger root (fresh)

- 1 cup peach (frozen)
- ½ teaspoon ground turmeric

Instructions
1. Place all of the ingredients in your blender, and blend until you get a creamy smoothie.

HEALTHY PINEAPPLE SMOOTHIE

Nutrition: Cal 126; Fat 3 g; Carb 19 g; Protein 4 g
Serving 1; Cook time 10 min

Ingredients
- ½ cup pineapple (frozen)
- 1 cup peach (frozen)
- 1 cup plain cashew yogurt
- 1 can pineapple chunks in juice

Instructions
1. Place all of the ingredients in your blender, and blend until you get a creamy smoothie.

WEIGHT GAIN SMOOTHIE

Nutrition: Cal 664; Fat 49 g; Carb 63 g; Protein 4 g
Serving 1; Cook time 10 min

Ingredients
- 1 cup pineapple (frozen)
- 1 banana (frozen)
- 1 cup coconut milk (chilled)
- ¼ cup pineapple juice (chilled)
- 1 tablespoon coconut flakes

Instructions
1. Place all of the ingredients in your blender, and blend until you get a creamy smoothie.

HEALTHY BLUEBERRY SMOOTHIE

Nutrition: Cal 237; Fat 3 g; Carb 42 g; Protein 4 g
Serving 1; Cook time 10 min

Ingredients
- 1 cup blueberries (frozen)
- 1 cup cashew milk
- ½ cup cashew yogurt (unsweetened plain)
- ½ banana

Instructions
1. Place all of the ingredients in your blender, and blend until you get a creamy smoothie.

IMMUNE BOOSTING SMOOTHIE

Nutrition: Cal 260; Fat 3 g; Carb 55 g; Protein 4 g
Serving 1; Cook time 10 min

Ingredients
- ½ cup dragon fruit (frozen)
- ½ cup blackberries (frozen)
- 1 banana
- 1 cup coconut water
- 1 teaspoon black elderberry syrup

Instructions
1. Place all of the ingredients in your blender, and blend until you get a creamy smoothie.

RASPBERRY CHOCOLATE SMOOTHIE

Nutrition: Cal 391; Fat 3 g; Carb 28 g; Protein 34 g
Serving 1; Cook time 10 min

Ingredients
- 2 ripe peaches (quartered, pits removed*)
- ½ banana
- 1 handful spinach
- ½ cup raspberries
- 1 tablespoon almond or cashew nut butter
- 2 tablespoons raw cocoa powder
- 10 oz unsweetened almond, hemp or coconut milk
- 1 scoop or serving plant-based protein powder

Instructions
1. Place all of the ingredients in your blender, and blend until you get a creamy smoothie.

COCONUT CASHEW PROTEIN SMOOTHIE

Nutrition: Cal 315; Fat 3 g; Carb 26 g; Protein 14 g
Serving 1; Cook time 10 min

Ingredients
- ½ banana
- 1 tablespoon of cashew butter
- ¼ cup full-fat coconut milk
- scoops dairy-free PaleoMeal protein powder
- 1 scoop of Espresso Dynamic Greens
- 2-3 ice cubes

Instructions
1. Place all of the ingredients in your blender, and blend until you get a creamy smoothie.

POMEGRANATE AND BERRY HIGH-PROTEIN SMOOTHIE

Nutrition: Cal 380; Fat 3 g; Carb 47 g; Protein 16 g
Serving 1; Cook time 10 min

Ingredients
- (15.2-ounce) bottle Odwalla Vanilla Protein Shake
- cup raspberries, frozen
- ½ cup strawberries, frozen
- ½ cup blueberries, frozen
- ¼ cup Safeway Signature Farms fresh pomegranate seeds, plus extra
- 1,5 tablespoons ground flax seeds
- 1,5 tablespoons chia seeds
- 1 banana, sliced

Instructions
1. Place all of the ingredients in your blender, and blend until you get a creamy smoothie.

COFFEE PROTEIN SMOOTHIE

Nutrition: Cal 426; Fat 14 g; Carb 32 g; Protein 4 g
Serving 1; Cook time 10 min

Ingredients
- medium frozen banana (100 grams)
- 1 cup frozen cauliflower rice (100 grams)
- 1 serving vanilla protein powder (I used whey protein)
- 1 tablespoon cashew butter
- 1 tablespoon chia seeds
- 1/2 teaspoon cinnamon
- 1/2 cup cold brew coffee (or more depending on desired thickness of smoothie)

Instructions
1. Place all of the ingredients in your blender, and blend until you get a creamy smoothie.

STRAWBERRY PROTEIN

Nutrition: Cal 206; Fat 2 g; Carb 28 g; Protein 4 g
Serving 1; Cook time 10 min

Ingredients
- 2 cups whole frozen strawberries
- 1/2 cup frozen sliced banana
- 1/4 cup vanilla protein powder (any kind will work)
- 1/3 cup nonfat Greek yogurt
- 1 cup unsweetened almond milk
- Optional topping: crushed graham crackers

Instructions
1. Place all of the ingredients in your blender, and blend until you get a creamy smoothie.

STRAWBERRY PROTEIN SMOOTHIE

Nutrition: Cal 135; Fat 3 g; Carb 13 g; Protein 13 g
Serving 1; Cook time 10 min

Ingredients
- 2 cups almond milk or any plant based milk
- 2 cups strawberries frozen
- 1/4 cup protein powder

Instructions
1. Place all of the ingredients in your blender, and blend until you get a creamy smoothie.

VANILLA PROTEIN SMOOTHIE

Nutrition: Cal 279; Fat 3 g; Carb 33 g; Protein 4 g
Serving 1; Cook time 10 min

Ingredients
- 1 cup frozen pineapple
- 1 banana (room temperature)
- 1 tablespoons peanut butter
- ½ cup Greek yogurt
- ½ cup milk (or almond milk or oat milk)
- ½ teaspoon vanilla extract
- 8 ice cubes

Instructions
1. Place all of the ingredients in your blender, and blend until you get a creamy smoothie.

MANGO SMOOTHIE WITH YOGURT

Nutrition: Cal 236; Fat 3 g; Carb 30 g; Protein 24 g
Serving 1; Cook time 10 min

Ingredients
- 1 cup mango frozen or fresh

- ½ cup nonfat Greek yogurt
- ½ cup almond milk
- ¼ cup vanilla protein powder optional

Instructions
1. Place all of the ingredients in your blender, and blend until you get a creamy smoothie.

CITRUS KIWI SMOOTHIE

Nutrition: Cal 317; Fat 3 g; Carb 77 g; Protein 4 g
Serving 1; Cook time 10 min

Ingredients
- 1 cup kale
- 2 oranges (cut into wedges)
- 1 cup strawberries (frozen)
- 1 kiwi (peeled)
- ½ banana
- 1 tbsp lemon (juice)

Instructions
1. Place all of the ingredients in your blender, and blend until you get a creamy smoothie.

PEAR SMOOTHIE

Nutrition: Cal 138; Fat 3 g; Carb 36 g; Protein 4 g
Serving 1; Cook time 10 min

Ingredients
- 1 cup spinach
- 1 cup water
- 1 pear (ripe)
- ½ cup peach (frozen)

Instructions
1. Place all of the ingredients in your blender, and blend until you get a creamy smoothie.

COCONUT OIL SMOOTHIE

Nutrition: Cal 289; Fat 3 g; Carb 41 g; Protein 4 g
Serving 1; Cook time 10 min

Ingredients
- 2 ripe peaches (quartered, pits removed*)
- 1 cup kale (fresh)
- 1 cup water
- 1 cup pineapple (frozen)
- ½ banana
- 1 tablespoon coconut oil

Instructions
1. Place all of the ingredients in your blender, and blend until you get a creamy smoothie.

FRUIT AND VEGETABLE SMOOTHIE

Nutrition: Cal 176; Fat 3 g; Carb 44g; Protein 5 g
Serving 1; Cook time 10 min

Ingredients
- ½ cup spinach
- ½ cup kale
- 1 apple (green)
- ½ cucumber (peeled)
- 1 lemon
- 1 celery (stalk)
- 1 inch ginger root
- 1 cup water

Instructions
1. Place all of the ingredients in your blender, and blend until you get a creamy smoothie.

SLEEP WELL SMOOTHIE

Nutrition: Cal 351; Fat 3 g; Carb 60 g; Protein 4 g
Serving 1; Cook time 10 min

Ingredients
- ¼ cup rolled oats (uncooked old-fashioned)
- 1 cup spinach
- ½ cup brewed chamomile tea (cooled)
- ½ cup Montmorency tart cherry juice (or more tea)
- 1 banana (fresh or frozen)
- 1 tablespoon almond butter

Instructions
1. Place all of the ingredients in your blender, and blend until you get a creamy smoothie.

CHOCOLATE PROTEIN SMOOTHIE

Nutrition: Cal 293; Fat 3 g; Carb 30 g; Protein 4 g
Serving 1; Cook time 10 min

Ingredients
- 3/4 cup unsweetened vanilla almond milk
- scoop (1/4 cup + 1 tablespoon (32g)) chocolate protein powder use a good-quality brand
- 1 tablespoon Dutch-process cocoa powder (Hershey's Special Dark works well)
- 1/2 cup frozen banana Note 1
- 1 tablespoon almond butter or peanut butter
- 1/4 teaspoon vanilla extract, optional
- 8 ice cubes

Instructions
1. Place all of the ingredients in your blender, and blend until you get a creamy smoothie.

RED BERRY PROTEIN SMOOTHIE

Nutrition: Cal 189; Fat 3 g; Carb 286g; Protein 8g
Serving 1; Cook time 10 min

Ingredients
- 2 cups frozen strawberries
- 2 cups frozen raspberries
- 2 cups plant based milk of choice
- ¼ cup canned white beans no salt added, drained and rinsed
- 2 tablespoon chopped fresh mint
- 1 tablespoon hemp seeds
- 1 tablespoon maple syrup or honey

Instructions

1. Place all of the ingredients in your blender, and blend until you get a creamy smoothie.

PROTEIN SMOOTHIE

Nutrition: Cal 263; Fat 3 g; Carb 27 g; Protein 25 g
Serving 1; Cook time 10 min

Ingredients
- 10 ounces mixed berries
- ½ cup Greek yogurt unsweetened
- scoop protein powder
- 1 tablespoon peanut butte
- ½ cup milk of choice

Instructions
1. Puree yogurt with juice in a blender until smooth. With the motor running, add fruit through the hole in the lid and continue to puree until smooth.

OATMEAL PROTEIN SMOOTHIE

Nutrition: Cal 290; Fat 3 g; Carb 43 g; Protein 4 g
Serving 1; Cook time 10 min

Ingredients
- 1 frozen banana, (chopped into chunks)
- ½ cup unsweetened almond milk, or oat milk, plus more as needed to reach desired consistency
- 2 Tablespoons old fashioned rolled oats
- 1 scoop (25 grams) vanilla protein powder
- ½ teaspoon cinnamon
- ½ teaspoon pure vanilla extract

Instructions
1. Place all of the ingredients in your blender, and blend until you get a creamy smoothie.

SNICKERDOODLE PROTEIN SMOOTHIE

Nutrition: Cal 263; Fat 3 g; Carb 27 g; Protein 4 g
Serving 1; Cook time 10 min

Ingredients
- cup ice
- 1/2 banana
- 1/2 cup almond milk
- 1 scoop vanilla protein (30g)
- 1 tsp almond butter
- 1/4 cup egg white (from a container so it's pasturized)
- 1 tsp vanilla
- 1 tsp cinnamon
- 1/2 tsp xantham gum

- **Instructions**
1. Place all of the ingredients in your blender, and blend until you get a creamy smoothie.

MORNING SMOOTHIE

Nutrition: Cal 414; Fat 3 g; Carb 19 g; Protein 11 g
Serving 1; Cook time 10 min

Ingredients
- 2 tablespoons oats any kind or gluten free
- tablespoon chia seeds or 2 tablespoons if you have pre-soaked chia seeds
- tablespoons cream cheese dairy or plant based
- 1 tablespoon oil vegetable, sunflower or groundnut
- 1 egg raw or hard boiled
- 1/2 teaspoon vanilla essence
- 1 teaspoon brown sugar honey or maple syrup

Instructions
1. Place all of the ingredients in your blender, and blend until you get a creamy smoothie.

ALMOND BUTTER & BANANA PROTEIN SMOOTHIE

Nutrition: Cal 402; Fat 3 g; Carb 37 g; Protein 19 g
Serving 1; Cook time 10 min

Ingredients
- small frozen banana
- 1 cup unsweetened almond milk
- tablespoons almond butter
- tablespoons unflavored protein powder
- 1 tablespoon sweetener of your choice (optional)
- ½ teaspoon ground cinnamon

Instructions
1. Place all of the ingredients in your blender, and blend until you get a creamy smoothie.

BERRY SPINACH PROTEIN SMOOTHIE

Nutrition: Cal 277; Fat 3 g; Carb 44 g; Protein 4 g
Serving 1; Cook time 10 min

Ingredients
- cup mixed berries (frozen)
- ½ banana
- ½ cup Greek yogurt (0% fat)
- 1 scoop protein powder
- ½ cup water
- 1 tablespoon flax seed meal
- 1 teaspoon grated fresh ginger (optional)
- 1 teaspoon cinnamon
- cups baby spinach
- handful ice

Instructions
1. Place all of the ingredients in your blender, and blend until you get a creamy smoothie.

FOR HEALTHY PROTEIN SMOOTHIES

Nutrition: Cal 364; Fat 3 g; Carb 45 g; Protein 4 g
Serving 1; Cook time 10 min

Ingredients
- 1 cup Almond Milk Plus Protein , divided (I used So Delicious brand with 5g added protein)
- 1/4 cup quick oats
- 1 (5.3) oz Strawberry or Blueberry Nonfat Greek Yogurt
- 1/2 overripe banana , chilled
- 1/2 cup fresh blueberries , chilled
- 5-6 ice cubes

Instructions
1. Place all of the ingredients in your blender, and blend until you get a creamy smoothie.

PINA COLADA SMOOTHIE

Nutrition: Cal 203; Fat 3 g; Carb 24 g; Protein 10 g
Serving 1; Co6k time 10 min

Ingredients
- 1 cup Almond Milk Plus Protein , divided
- 1/4 cup quick oats
- 1 (5.3) oz Vanilla or Strawberry Nonfat Greek Yogurt
- 1/2 overripe banana , chilled
- 1/2 cup diced fresh pineapple , chilled
- 1/4 tsp coconut extract
- 5-6 ice cubes

Instructions
1. Place all of the ingredients in your blender, and blend until you get a creamy smoothie.

HIGH PROTEIN BLUEBERRY KALE SMOOTHIE

Nutrition: Cal 240; Fat 3 g; Carb 37 g; Protein 17 g
Serving 1; Cook time 10 min

Ingredients
- ½ banana
- ½ cup chopped kale
- ½ cup blueberries (fresh or frozen)
- ½ cup plain low fat yogurt
- 1 scoop protein powder (1/2 c water optional)
- 1 tablespoon flax seed meal
- ½ teaspoon cinnamon
- two handfuls ice or more to taste

Instructions
1. Place all of the ingredients in your blender, and blend until you get a creamy smoothie.

BANANA OATMEAL SMOOTHIE

Nutrition: Cal 449; Fat 3 g; Carb 65g; Protein 4 g
Serving 1; Cook time 10 min

Ingredients
- ½ cup rolled oats
- cup coconut milk
- 1 banana (frozen)
- ½ teaspoon ground cinnamon
- 1 teaspoon vanilla extract
- ½ teaspoon maple syrup (optional)

Instructions
1. Place all of the ingredients in your blender, and blend until you get a creamy smoothie.

CREAMY BLACKBERRY SMOOTHIE

Nutrition: Cal 288; Fat 3 g; Carb 35 g; Protein 4 g
Serving 1; Cook time 10 min

Ingredients
- 1 cup spinach
- 1 cup coconut milk
- 1 cup blackberries
- ½ banana

Instructions
1. Place all of the ingredients in your blender, and blend until you get a creamy smoothie.

HOLIDAY CRANBERRY SMOOTHIE

Nutrition: Cal 144; Fat 3 g; Carb 36 g; Protein 4 g
Serving 1; Cook time 10 min

Ingredients
- cup spinach
- 1 cup water
- ½ cup cranberries
- 1 orange (peeled)
- ½ banana (frozen)

Instructions
1. Place all of the ingredients in your blender, and blend until you get a creamy smoothie.

CINNAMON DATE SMOOTHIE

Nutrition: Cal 421; Fat 7 g; Carb 86g; Protein 4 g
Serving 1; Cook time 10 min

Ingredients
- ½ cup rolled oats
- 3 medjool dates (pitted)
- ½ cups plant milk (ex: cashew, almond, or oat)
- ½ teaspoon vanilla extract
- teaspoon ground cinnamon

Instructions
1. Place all of the ingredients in your blender, and blend until you get a creamy smoothie.

FAT BURNING SMOOTHIE FOR WEIGHT LOSS

Nutrition: Cal 231; Fat 3 g; Carb 42 g; Protein 4 g
Serving 1; Cook time 10 min

Ingredients
- 1 cup spinach
- 1 tablespoon fresh mint
- 1 stalk celery (chopped)
- ½ cup brewed green tea (cooled)
- ½ grapefruit (peeled and seeded)

- 1 cup pineapple (frozen)
- ¼ avocado
- dash cayenne pepper (optional)

Instructions
1. Place all of the ingredients in your blender, and blend until you get a creamy smoothie.

CHOCOLATE PEANUT BUTTER SMOOTHIE

Nutrition: Cal 497; Fat 15 g; Carb 90 g; Protein 4 g
Serving 1; Cook time 10 min

Ingredients
- 2 bananas (frozen)
- tablespoon peanut butter
- tablespoon cacao powder
- 1 cup oat milk (or another plant milk)
- 1 teaspoon ground cinnamon (optional)

Instructions
1. Place all of the ingredients in your blender, and blend until you get a creamy smoothie.

DARK CHOCOLATE BANANA NUT

Nutrition: Cal 229; Fat 3 g; Carb 26 g; Protein 28 g
Serving 1; Cook time 10 min

Ingredients
- ½ banana
- teaspoon dark chocolate morsels (dairy-free)
- ⅛ cup chopped walnuts
- 1 cup unsweetened almond milk
- 6 ice cubes
- ⅓ cup chocolate plant-based protein powder
- Water to blend (optional)

Instructions
1. Place all of the ingredients in your blender, and blend until you get a creamy smoothie.

AB OF STEEL

Nutrition: Cal 340; Fat 3 g; Carb 36 g; Protein 20 g
Serving 1; Cook time 10 min

Ingredients
- ¾ frozen banana
- 2 teaspoons almond butter
- ¾ cup unsweetened almond milk
- scoop chocolate or vanilla plant-based protein powder

Instructions
1. Place all of the ingredients in your blender, and blend until you get a creamy smoothie.

BLACK AND BLUE BERRY VANILLA PROTEIN SMOOTHIE

Nutrition: Cal 233; Fat 11 g; Carb 39 g; Protein 4 g
Serving 1; Cook time 10 min

Ingredients
- 3/4 C milk {whole or 2%}
- 1/8 teaspoon pure vanilla extract
- Cup {total} frozen blackberries and blueberries

- 1 scoop of your favorite powdered vanilla-flavored protein drink
- tsp agave nectar, you could also use honey

Instructions
1. Place all of the ingredients in your blender, and blend until you get a creamy smoothie.

SUPER THICK BLUEBERRY SMOOTHIE

Nutrition: Cal 603; Fat 3 g; Carb 37 g; Protein 4 g
Serving 1; Cook time 10 min

Ingredients
- handful of ice (about 5 large cubes)
- 1/2 medium banana, frozen
- 1/2 cup almond milk
- 2/3 cup frozen blueberries
- 1 handful spinach leaves (optional)
- 1 scoop of vanilla protein powder (optional)
- Optional toppings: Almonds, blueberries, chia seeds, etc

Instructions
1. Place all of the ingredients in your blender, and blend until you get a creamy smoothie.

CHOCOLATE DECADENCE

Nutrition: Cal 300; Fat 3 g; Carb 34 g; Protein 4 g
Serving 1; Cook time 10 min

Ingredients
- ½ banana
- ¼ ripe avocado, peeled, pitted, and quartered
- ¼ cup black beans
- ½ cup unsweetened almond milk
- ¼ cup chocolate plant-based protein powder
- 6 ice cubes
- Water to blend

Instructions
1. Place all of the ingredients in your blender, and blend until you get a creamy smoothie.

TABASCO CHERRY

Nutrition: Cal 232; Fat 2 g; Carb 28 g; Protein 26 g
Serving 1; Cook time 10 min

Ingredients
- ½ cup cherries
- ½ frozen banana
- 1 tsp Tabasco sauce
- ¼ lime
- ¼ cup unsweetened almond milk
- 1 scoop plant-based plain protein powder
- 3 ice cubes
- Water to blend (optional)

Instructions
1. Place all of the ingredients in your blender, and blend until you get a creamy smoothie.

ORANGE CREAMSICLE SMOOTHIE

Nutrition: Cal 90; Fat 10 g; Carb 37 g; Protein 4 g
Serving 1; Cook time 10 min

Ingredients
- cup frozen banana slices
- 1 teaspoon vanilla extract
- 1 cup 100% orange juice
- optional: 1/2 cup ice
- optional: 1 scoop vanilla protein powder, coconut whipped cream, orange zest

Instructions
1. Place all of the ingredients in your blender, and blend until you get a creamy smoothie.

ALMOND GINGER BLUEBERRY ANTI-INFLAMMATORY SMOOTHIE

Nutrition: Cal 331; Fat 17 g; Carb 22 g; Protein 4 g
Serving 1; Cook time 10 min

Ingredients
- 1/4 cup frozen blueberries
- cup frozen, chopped spinach
- 1 teaspoon minced fresh ginger (or could use 1/2 teaspoon ground ginger)
- 1 Tablespoon almond butter
- 1 Tablespoon ground flaxseed
- 1 scoop vanilla protein powder (my favorite is the Vega protein powder)
- 1 cup unsweetened almond milk

Instructions
1. Place all of the ingredients in your blender, and blend until you get a creamy smoothie.

PEACH OAT SMOOTHIE

Nutrition: Cal 142; Fat 3 g; Carb 28 g; Protein 4 g
Serving 1; Cook time 10 min

Ingredients
- 2 ripe peaches (quartered, pits removed*)
- 1 Tbsp chia seeds
- 1/4 cup rolled oats (gluten-free for GF eaters)
- 1/2 frozen banana (peeled before freezing)
- 1/4 cup fresh orange juice
- 1/2 cup unsweetened almond milk
- 1 Tbsp agave, maple syrup, or a pinch of stevia (*optional /for added sweetness / or honey for non-vegan*

Instructions
1. Place all of the ingredients in your blender, and blend until you get a creamy smoothie.

CHOCOLATE BEET SMOOTHIE

Nutrition: Cal 90; Fat 3 g; Carb 37 g; Protein 4 g
Serving 1; Cook time 10 min

Ingredients
- 1/4-1/2 cup unsweetened vanilla almond milk (depending on desired consistency)
- 3/4 cup plain greek yogurt (used Siggi's 0%)
- cup diced cooked beets* (150 grams/2-3 small-medium)
- 1 cup frozen cauliflower rice
- heaping tablespoons cacao powder
- 1 tablespoon cashew butter
- 1 teaspoon honey
- 1/2 teaspoon cinnamon
- 1 scoop chocolate protein powder (optional)

Instructions
1. Place all of the ingredients in your blender, and blend until you get a creamy smoothie.

ANTI INFLAMMATORY BERRY GINGER SMOOTHIE

Nutrition: Cal 328; Fat 3 g; Carb 24 g; Protein 20 g
Serving 1; Cook time 10 min

Ingredients
- 1 cup frozen berry blend (blueberries, raspberries, cherries)
- 1/2 cup frozen riced cauliflower (or frozen grated zucchini)
- 1/2 tsp cinnamon + dash of ginger (fresh or ground)
- 1 Tbsp. apple cider vinegar
- 1/2 cup vanilla cashew milk (or almond milk)
- 1 scoop bone broth vanilla protein*
- Handful of spinach (optional)
- 1 Tbsp. almond butter

Instructions
1. Place all of the ingredients in your blender, and blend until you get a creamy smoothie.

POWER BREAKFAST SMOOTHIE

Nutrition: Cal 200; Fat 3 g; Carb 34 g; Protein 6 g
Serving 1; Cook time 10 min

Ingredients
- 1 cup spinach
- 1 cup Almond Breeze Original Almondmilk
- ½ banana
- ¼ cup blueberries
- 1,5 tablespoons rolled oats
- 1,5 tablespoons almond butter
- 2 servings protein powder
- ¼ cup water, optional
- ice

Instructions
1. Place all of the ingredients in your blender, and blend until you get a creamy smoothie.

BLUEBERRY SMOOTHIE

Nutrition: Cal 370; Fat 3 g; Carb 28 g; Protein 25 g
Serving 1; Cook time 10 min

Ingredients
- 1 c. frozen blueberries
- 1/2 c. unsweetened almond milk
- 1 1/2 scoops protein powder
- tbsp. unsweetened almond butter

- 1 tsp. pure vanilla extract
- 1/2 c. fresh blueberries
- 1/4 c. vanilla granola
- tbsp. sliced almonds
- 2 tsp. hemp seeds
- 1 tsp. ground cinnamon

Instructions
1. Place all of the ingredients in your blender, and blend until you get a creamy smoothie.

STICKY DATE SMOOTHIE

Nutrition: Cal 241; Fat 6 g; Carb 35 g; Protein 4 g
Serving 1; Cook time 10 min

Ingredients
- 1/2 bananas, frozen
- 3 Medjool dates, pitted
- 1/4 avocado
- 1 cup almond milk
- 1/2 teaspoon maca
- 1/2 teaspoon cinnamon
- 1/2 teaspoon vanilla extract, optional
- tablespoons protein powder

Instructions
1. Place all of the ingredients in your blender, and blend until you get a creamy smoothie.

MEAL REPLACEMENT SMOOTHIE

Nutrition: Cal 343; Fat 3 g; Carb 50 g; Protein 10 g
Serving 1; Cook time 10 min

Ingredients
- 1 cup kale (or spinach)
- 1 cup almond milk (unsweetened)
- 1 cup blueberries (frozen)
- 1 banana
- 1 tablespoon almond butter (or raw almonds)
- tablespoon rolled oats

Instructions
1. Place all of the ingredients in your blender, and blend until you get a creamy smoothie.

OAT AND BERRY SMOOTHIE

Nutrition: Cal 148; Fat 3 g; Carb 21 g; Protein 5 g
Serving 1; Cook time 10 min

Ingredients
- 1/2 cup Fresh 'n Fruity Fruit of the Forest yoghurt
- 1/4 cup Rolled oats
- 1/2 cup Anchor Protein+ milk
- 1/4 cup Mixed berries

Instructions
1. Place all of the ingredients in your blender, and blend until you get a creamy smoothie.

MANGO SMOOTHIE

Nutrition: Cal 222; Fat 7g; Carb 28 g; Protein 4 g
Serving 1; Cook time 10 min

Ingredients
- 1 cup mango (frozen)
- ½ cup cashew milk
- ½ cup cashew yogurt (plain)
- ½ teaspoon ground turmeric
- ½ orange (peeled)

Instructions
1. Place all of the ingredients in your blender, and blend until you get a creamy smoothie.

HEMP CAT

Nutrition: Cal 270; Fat 3 g; Carb 26 g; Protein 4 g
Serving 1; Cook time 10 min

Ingredients
- ¾ cup baby kale
- ½ frozen banana
- teaspoon hemp seeds
- ½ tablespoon chia seeds
- ½ cup unsweetened almond milk
- 1 scoop vanilla plant-based protein powder
- Water to blend (optional)

Instructions
1. Place all of the ingredients in your blender, and blend until you get a creamy smoothie.

WARM CHAI SMOOTHIE

Nutrition: Cal 396; Fat 25 g; Carb 35 g; Protein 4 g
Serving 1; Cook time 10 min

Ingredients
- ½ cup spinach
- ½ cup brewed tea (herbal green, white or black)
- ½ cup **coconut milk**
- ½ pear (cored and peeled)
- ½ apple (cored and peeled)
- medjool date
- ½ teaspoon ground cinnamon
- ¼ inch ginger root
- ⅛ teaspoon ground cardamom

Instructions
1. Place all of the ingredients in your blender, and blend until you get a creamy smoothie.

CHERRY SMOOTHIE

Nutrition: Cal 291; Fat 3 g; Carb 68 g; Protein 4 g
Serving 1; Cook time 10 min

Ingredients
- cup sweet pitted cherries
- 1/2 banana
- 1 cup nonfat milk
- 1 tablespoon honey

- 1/4 teaspoon vanilla extract
- 1/4 teaspoon cinnamon
- 1/2 cup ice

Instructions

1. Place all of the ingredients in your blender, and blend until you get a creamy smoothie.

VEGAN BREAKFAST SMOOTHIE

Nutrition: Cal 115; Fat 3 g; Carb 28 g; Protein 12 g
Serving 1; Cook time 10 min

Ingredients

- 1 cup berries frozen
- 1/4 cup protein powder
- 1 1/2 cups unsweetened almond milk or any plant based milk
- 1 tbsp peanut butter optional
- Add all your ingredients into a high speed blender and blend until thick and creamy.

Instructions

1. Place all of the ingredients in your blender, and blend until you get a creamy smoothie.

PEANUT BUTTER BANANA SMOOTHIE

Nutrition: Cal 380; Fat 3 g; Carb 23 g; Protein 4 g
Serving 1; Cook time 10 min

Ingredients

- 1/4 cup unsweetened almond milk
- 1 large banana cut into chunks and frozen
- 1,5 tablespoons creamy peanut butter
- 1/2 cup nonfat plain Greek yogurt
- 1/4 teaspoon ground cinnamon
- Ice

Instructions

1. Place all of the ingredients in your blender, and blend until you get a creamy smoothie.

FIESTA SAVORY SMOOTHIE

Nutrition: Cal 270; Fat 3 g; Carb 40 g; Protein 7 g
Serving 1; Cook time 10 min

Ingredients

- cup spinach
- ½ cup fresh cilantro
- 1 cup vegetable stock
- ½ cup chickpeas (canned (drained))
- ½ cup tomato (fresh (diced))
- ¼ avocado
- 1 serving Protein Smoothie Boost
- ½ lemon (juiced)
- ½ teaspoon chili powder
- ¼ teaspoon cumin (ground)
- 1 pinch cayenne pepper
- 1 pinch sea salt
- 1 pinch black pepper

Instructions

1. Place all of the ingredients in your blender, and blend until you get a creamy smoothie.

CREAMY BANANA SMOOTHIE

Nutrition: Cal 142; Fat 3 g; Carb 28 g; Protein 4 g
Serving 1; Cook time 10 min

Ingredients

- 2 bananas (frozen)
- 1/2 cup cashew yogurt (plain or vanilla)
- 1 cup cashew milk
- 1 serving collagen powder (or 1 serving Protein Smoothie Boost)
- 1 teaspoon vanilla extract

Instructions

1. Place all of the ingredients in your blender, and blend until you get a creamy smoothie.

BUTTERNUT SQUASH SMOOTHIE

Nutrition: Cal 380; Fat 3 g; Carb 38 g; Protein 4 g
Serving 1; Cook time 10 min

Ingredients

- ¾ cups spinach
- 1 cup cashew milk (warmed)
- ¾ cup butternut squash (cooked (see notes))
- ½ pear (peeled and cored)
- ¼ teaspoon ground cinnamon
- ¼ teaspoon ground nutmeg

Instructions

1. Place all of the ingredients in your blender, and blend until you get a creamy smoothie.

CREAMY AVOCADO SMOOTHIE

Nutrition: Cal 331; Fat 3 g; Carb 23 g; Protein 6 g
Serving 1; Cook time 10 min

Ingredients

- 1cup cashew milk
- 1 cup spinach
- 1 tablespoon raw cashews
- ½ avocado
- 1 cup pineapple (frozen)

Instructions

1. Place all of the ingredients in your blender, and blend until you get a creamy smoothie.

ALMOND BUTTER SMOOTHIE

Nutrition: Cal 448; Fat 22 g; Carb 28 g; Protein 11 g
Serving 1; Cook time 10 min

Ingredients

- 1 cup spinach
- 1 cup almond milk
- 1 cup grapes (red)
- 1 banana
- 1 tablespoon almond butter

Instructions

1. Place all of the ingredients in your blender, and blend until you get a creamy smoothie.

ORANGE JULIUS SMOOTHIE

Nutrition: Cal 147; Fat 3 g; Carb 34 g; Protein 4 g
Serving 1; Cook time 10 min

Ingredients
- 1 cup spinach
- ¼ cup almond milk
- 2 oranges
- ½ banana (frozen)

Instructions
1. Place all of the ingredients in your blender, and blend until you get a creamy smoothie.

SMOOTHIE FOR BLOATING

Nutrition: Cal 145; Fat 3 g; Carb 34 g; Protein 3 g
Serving 1; Cook time 10 min

Ingredients
- 1 cup spinach
- ½ cucumber (peeled if desired)
- 1 stalk celery
- 1 cup pineapple (frozen)
- ¼ cup papaya
- 1 tablespoon ginger root (fresh)
- 1 tablespoon lime (juice)

Instructions
1. Place all of the ingredients in your blender, and blend until you get a creamy smoothie.

SUMMER MELON SMOOTHIE

Nutrition: Cal 102; Fat 3 g; Carb 25 g; Protein 4 g
Serving 1; Cook time 10 min

Ingredients
- 1 cup spinach
- 1 ½ cups watermelon (chilled)
- ¼ cup strawberries (frozen)
- ¼ cup blackberries

Instructions
1. Place all of the ingredients in your blender, and blend until you get a creamy smoothie.

ADRENAL FATIGUE DIET SMOOTHIE

Nutrition: Cal 130; Fat 3 g; Carb 34 g; Protein 4 g
Serving 1; Cook time 10 min

Ingredients
- 1 cup spinach
- ½ cup coconut water
- ½ orange (peeled)
- 1 cup pineapple (fresh or frozen)
- ½ cup cauliflower florets (frozen)
- 1 tablespoon fresh turmeric (or 1 teaspoon ground turmeric)
- 1 tablespoon flaxseed oil
- adaptogenic herbs

Instructions
1. Place all of the ingredients in your blender, and blend until you get a creamy smoothie.

BEST GREEN PROTEIN SMOOTHIE

Nutrition: Cal 154; Fat 3 g; Carb 25 g; Protein 4 g
Serving 1; Cook time 10 min

Ingredients
- 1 cup spinach
- 1 cup water
- ½ cup pineapple (frozen)
- ½ cup mango (frozen)
- 1 banana

Instructions
1. Place all of the ingredients in your blender, and blend until you get a creamy smoothie.

MCT OIL SMOOTHIE

Nutrition: Cal 142; Fat 3 g; Carb 28 g; Protein 4 g
Serving 1; Cook time 10 min

Ingredients
- 1 cup spinach
- 1 tablespoon cilantro (fresh)
- 1 inch ginger root
- ½ cup water
- 1 cup cucumber (diced + peeled)
- 1 apple (green, cored + peeled)
- 1 tablespoon lemon (juice)
- 1 teaspoon MCT oil

Instructions
1. Place all of the ingredients in your blender, and blend until you get a creamy smoothie.

CHERRY BEET SMOOTHIE

Nutrition: Cal 172; Fat 3 g; Carb 50 g; Protein 3 g
Serving 1; Cook time 10 min

Ingredients
- ¼ cup beet (peeled and diced)
- 1 cup cherries
- ¼ banana (frozen)
- ½ cup pomegranate juice
- ½ cup water
- fresh mint (for garnish)

Instructions
1. Place all of the ingredients in your blender, and blend until you get a creamy smoothie.

GREEN ENERGY SMOOTHIE

Nutrition: Cal 148; Fat 3 g; Carb 40 g; Protein 4 g
Serving 1; Cook time 10 min

Ingredients
- 1 cup spinach
- ½ cup water
- ½ grapefruit (peeled)

- 1 cup pineapple (frozen)

Instructions
1. Place all of the ingredients in your blender, and blend until you get a creamy smoothie

BLUEBERRY CHIA SMOOTHIE

Nutrition: Cal 160; Fat 3 g; Carb 45 g; Protein 4 g
Serving 1; Cook time 10 min

Ingredients
- 1 cup blueberries
- 1/2 banana
- 1/2 cup nonfat milk
- 1/2 cup plain nonfat Greek Yogurt
- 1 tablespoon chia seeds
- 1/2 cup ice

Instructions
1. Place all of the ingredients in your blender, and blend until you get a creamy smoothie.

APPLE CELERY SMOOTHIE

Nutrition: Cal 227; Fat 3 g; Carb 57 g; Protein 4 g
Serving 1; Cook time 10 min

Ingredients
- 1 cup spinach
- 1 cup water
- ¼ fennel bulb (cored and roughly chopped*)
- 1 stalk celery
- 1 apple (green, cored)
- 1/4 inch ginger root
- 1 lemon (peeled)

Instructions
1. Place all of the ingredients in your blender, and blend until you get a creamy smoothie.

STRAWBERRY OAT SMOOTHIE

Nutrition: Cal 142; Fat 3 g; Carb 28 g; Protein 4 g
Serving 1; Cook time 10 min

Ingredients
- 1 cup sliced strawberries
- 1/2 banana
- 1 cup nonfat milk
- 1/4 cup rolled oats
- 1 teaspoon honey
- 1/4 teaspoon vanilla
- 1/2 cup ice

Instructions
1. Place all of the ingredients in your blender, and blend until you get a creamy smoothie.

WATERMELON MINT SMOOTHIE

Nutrition: Cal 142; Fat 3 g; Carb 28 g; Protein 4 g
Serving 1; Cook time 10 min

Ingredients
- 2 cups watermelon chunks (use seedless watermelon or remove the seeds)
- 1/2 tablespoon fresh mint
- 1/2 cup plain nonfat Greek yogurt
- 1 tablespoon honey
- 1/2 cup ice

Instructions
1. Place all of the ingredients in your blender, and blend until you get a creamy smoothie.

ANTI-INFLAMMATORY CHERRY-SPINACH SMOOTHIE

Nutrition: Cal 440; Fat 3 g; Carb 30 g; Protein 4 g
Serving 1; Cook time 10 min

Ingredients
- 1 cup plain low-fat kefir
- 1 cup frozen cherries
- 1/2 cup baby spinach leaves
- ¼ cup mashed ripe avocado
- 1 tablespoon salted almond butter
- 1 (1/2 inch) piece peeled ginger
- 1 teaspoon chia seeds, plus more for garnish

Instructions
1. Place all of the ingredients in your blender, and blend until you get a creamy smoothie.

MANGO RASPBERRY SMOOTHIE

Nutrition: Cal 198; Fat 3 g; Carb 35 g; Protein 4 g
Serving 1; Cook time 10 min

Ingredients
- 1/2 cup water
- 1/2 medium avocado
- 1 tablespoon lemon juice
- 3/4 cup frozen mango
- 1/4 cup frozen raspberries
- 1 tablespoon agave (Optional)

Instructions
1. Place all of the ingredients in your blender, and blend until you get a creamy smoothie.

CARROT-APPLE SMOOTHIE

Nutrition: Cal 243; Fat 3 g; Carb 46 g; Protein 4 g
Serving 1; Cook time 10 min

Ingredients
- 2 large carrots, sliced (about 1 1/2 cups)
- 1 medium-ripe banana
- 1 large Honeycrisp apple, cored and quartered
- 1 cup light coconut milk
- 2 tablespoons fresh lemon juice
- 2 teaspoons minced fresh ginger
- 2 teaspoons minced fresh turmeric or 1 teaspoon ground turmeric
- 1/2 cup ice cubes

Instructions
1. Place all of the ingredients in your blender, and blend until you get a creamy smoothie.

CITRUS-PINEAPPLE SMOOTHIE

Nutrition: Cal 133; Fat 3 g; Carb 48 g; Protein 4 g
Serving 1; Cook time 10 min

Ingredients
- Put 1/2 cup fat-free Greek yogurt
- 1/2 cup frozen pineapple chunks
- 1 tsp vanilla extract, 1/2 navel orange, segmented
- 1/2 ruby grapefruit, segmented

Instructions
1. Place all of the ingredients in your blender, and blend until you get a creamy smoothie.

BLUEBERRY & AVOCADO SMOOTHIE

Nutrition: Cal 188; Fat 3 g; Carb 34 g; Protein 4 g
Serving 1; Cook time 10 min

Ingredients
- 1 cup frozen blueberries
- 1/2 avocado, pitted and sliced
- 5 dates, pitted and roughly chopped
- 1 cup unsweetened vanilla coconut milk

Instructions
1. Place all of the ingredients in your blender, and blend until you get a creamy smoothie.

STRAWBERRY-MANGO-BANANA SMOOTHIE

Nutrition: Cal 299; Fat 3 g; Carb 42 g; Protein 4 g
Serving 1; Cook time 10 min

Ingredients
- 1/2 cup frozen strawberries
- 1/2 cup chopped ripe mango
- 1/2 medium ripe banana (frozen, if desired)
- 1/2 cup unsweetened refrigerated coconut milk beverage (such as So Delicious), plus more if needed
- 1 tablespoon cashew butter
- 1 tablespoon ground chia seeds

Instructions
1. Place all of the ingredients in your blender, and blend until you get a creamy smoothie.

CRANBERRY AND RASPBERRY SMOOTHIE

Nutrition: Cal 100; Fat 3 g; Carb 17 g; Protein 4 g
Serving 1; Cook time 10 min

Ingredients
- 1/2 cranberry juice
- 1/2 frozen raspberry, defrosted
- 1/2 milk
- 1/2 natural yogurt
- 1 tbsp caster sugar, or to taste

Instructions
1. Place all of the ingredients in your blender, and blend until you get a creamy smoothie.

HIGH IN VITAMIN C

Nutrition: Cal 52; Fat 3 g; Carb 13 g; Protein 4 g
Serving 1; Cook time 10 min

Ingredients
- 2 oranges (peeled and halved)
- 1 cup papaya (cubed or sliced)
- 1 cup pineapple (cubed)
- 1 mango (cubed)
- 1 cup orange cauliflower florets (see notes)

Instructions
1. Place all of the ingredients in your blender, and blend until you get a creamy smoothie.

BERRY-KEFIR SMOOTHIE

Nutrition: Cal 304; Fat 3 g; Carb 53 g; Protein 4 g
Serving 1; Cook time 10 min

Ingredients
- 1 1/2 cups frozen mixed berries
- 1 cup plain kefir
- 1/2 medium banana
- 2 teaspoons almond butter
- 1/2 teaspoon vanilla extract

Instructions
1. Place all of the ingredients in your blender, and blend until you get a creamy smoothie.

MANGO COLADA SMOOTHIE

Nutrition: Cal 142; Fat 3 g; Carb 28 g; Protein 4 g
Serving 1; Cook time 10 min

Ingredients
- 1 cup nonfat plain Greek yogurt
- 3/4 cup frozen pineapple
- 3/4 cup frozen mango
- 1/2 cup "lite" coconut milk (see Tip)
- Unsweetened coconut flakes for garnish

Instructions
1. Place all of the ingredients in your blender, and blend until you get a creamy smoothie.

PINEAPPLE BANANA SMOOTHIE

Nutrition: Cal 179; Fat 3 g; Carb 37 g; Protein 4 g
Serving 1; Cook time 10 min

Ingredients
- 1 cup spinach
- 1 cup almond milk (unsweetened)
- 1/2 cup pineapple (frozen)
- 1/2 cup cherries (frozen)
- 1/2 banana

Instructions
1. Place all of the ingredients in your blender, and blend until you get a creamy smoothie.

SMOOTHIE FOR PREGNANCY

Nutrition: Cal 231; Fat 3 g; Carb 45 g; Protein 4 g
Serving 1; Cook time 10 min

Ingredients
- 1 cup spinach
- 1 cup coconut water (unsweetened)
- 1/2 banana
- 1/2 cup pineapple (frozen)
- 1/2 cup carrot (uncooked)
- 1 tablespoon chia seeds

Instructions
1. Place all of the ingredients in your blender, and blend until you get a creamy smoothie.

PEACH RASPBERRY SMOOTHIE

Nutrition: Cal 247; Fat 3 g; Carb 55 g; Protein 4 g
Serving 1; Cook time 10 min

Ingredients
- 10 oz. fat free vanilla yogurt (or any kind of vanilla)
- 1/2 cup vanilla soy milk
- 1/2 cup frozen raspberries
- 3/4 cup frozen peaches
- 3/4 cup crushed ice
- 2 tablespoons honey

Instructions
1. Place all of the ingredients in your blender, and blend until you get a creamy smoothie.

PUMPKIN SMOOTHIE

Nutrition: Cal 236; Fat 3 g; Carb 44 g; Protein 4 g
Serving 1; Cook time 10 min

Ingredients
- 1/2 cup Greek yogurt or plain yogurt (or oat milk for vegan)
- 1/2 cup pumpkin puree
- medium ripe banana
- 1 1/2 cups fresh apple chunks (skin on, about 1 medium apple)
- 1 teaspoon Pumpkin Pie Spice
- 1 teaspoon vanilla extract
- 1 1/2 tablespoons maple syrup
- 1 cup ice cubes

Instructions
1. Place all of the ingredients in your blender, and blend until you get a creamy smoothie.

MOJITO SMOOTHIE

Nutrition: Cal 137; Fat 3 g; Carb 33 g; Protein 4 g
Serving 1; Cook time 10 min

Ingredients
- 1 cup frozen watermelon chunks (about 8–10 1" cubes)
- 1 cup frozen strawberries (about 6 large strawberries)
- 1 cup coconut water
- 1 teaspoon lime juice (or to taste)
- mint leaves (plus more for garnish)
- Sweetener such as honey or maple syrup (optional, to taste)

Instructions
1. Place all of the ingredients in your blender, and blend until you get a creamy smoothie.

COCONUT MILK SMOOTHIE

Nutrition: Cal 142; Fat 3 g; Carb 28 g; Protein 4 g
Serving 1; Cook time 10 min

Ingredients
- 2 cups frozen strawberries (or other frozen fruit: blueberries, mixed berries, pineapple, mango, etc)
- 2 bananas (room temperature)
- 1/2 cup full fat coconut milk
- 3/4 cup water
- 1/2 cup ice

Instructions
1. Place all of the ingredients in your blender, and blend until you get a creamy smoothie.

EASY BEET SMOOTHIE

Nutrition: Cal 163; Fat 3 g; Carb 39 g; Protein 2 g
Serving 1; Cook time 10 min

Ingredients
- 1 small raw beet (about 2/3 cup peeled and diced)
- 1 large green apple
- 1 banana
- 1 cup frozen pineapple chunks or mango
- 1/2 cup water
- 10 ice cubes

Instructions
1. Place all of the ingredients in your blender, and blend until you get a creamy smoothie.

BEST ALMOND MILK SMOOTHIE

Nutrition: Cal 280; Fat 3 g; Carb 37 g; Protein 4 g
Serving 1; Cook time 10 min

Ingredients
- 2 cups frozen strawberries
- 2 bananas (room temperature)
- 1/2 to 2/3 cup almond milk
- 8 ice cubes
- tablespoon almond butter (optional)

Instructions
1. Place all of the ingredients in your blender, and blend until you get a creamy smoothie.

BEST PEANUT BUTTER SMOOTHIE

Nutrition: Cal 280; Fat 3 g; Carb 36 g; Protein 4 g
Serving 1; Cook time 10 min

Ingredients
- 3 tablespoons peanut butter
- 2 medium ripe bananas (room temperature)
- ½ cups ice
- ¾ cup milk or nondairy milk (like almond, oat or coconut milk)

Instructions

1. Place all of the ingredients in your blender, and blend until you get a creamy smoothie.

CARROT SMOOTHIE

Nutrition: Cal 185; Fat 3 g; Carb 46 g; Protein 4 g
Serving 1; Cook time 10 min

Ingredients
- 1 cup thinly sliced carrot rounds
- 1 large apple, chopped into cubes
- 1 banana (room temperature)
- 1/2 cup orange juice*
- 1/2 cup frozen pineapple or mango
- 10 ice cubes
- Optional mix in: 1/2 teaspoon grated fresh ginger, ¼ teaspoon cinnamon

Instructions
1. Place all of the ingredients in your blender, and blend until you get a creamy smoothie.

NUTRIENT-DENSE SMOOTHIE

Nutrition: Cal 222; Fat 3 g; Carb 51 g; Protein 4 g
Serving 1; Cook time 10 min

Ingredients
- 4 cups kale, packed (approximately 4 leaves)
- 1 cup frozen blueberries (organic)
- 1 cup frozen raspberries (organic)
- 2/3 cup coconut yogurt or regular plain yogurt (8 oz)
- 1/2 cup raw beets (1 beet)
- 1 banana (optional or 1/2 banana)
- 1/2 cup filtered water (or 1 cup if you want it thinner)
- 4 scoops vital proteins collagen peptides (optional to add a protein source to the smoothie)

Instructions
1. Place all of the ingredients in your blender, and blend until you get a creamy smoothie.

BAHAMA MAMA SMOOTHIE

Nutrition: Cal 490; Fat 3 g; Carb 60 g; Protein 4 g
Serving 1; Cook time 10 min

Ingredients
- 1/2 cups/8 oz frozen strawberries
- 1/2 cups/8 oz frozen pineapple
- 1 cup/8 fl oz coconut milk (can sub for another milk of choice)
- 1 tbsp/1 oz white chocolate, chopped (or chocolate chips)
- 1 to 2 tbsp agave syrup (can sub for honey or maple syrup)

Instructions
1. Place all of the ingredients in your blender, and blend until you get a creamy smoothie.

MATCHA BANANA SMOOTHIE

Nutrition: Cal 462; Fat 3 g; Carb 49 g; Protein 4 g
Serving 1; Cook time 10 min

Ingredients
- 6 medium pitted dates (or 1/4 cup honey/agave)
- 1/4 cup almond butter
- 1 cup almond milk
- 1/4 cup matcha powder
- 1 medium frozen banana

Instructions
1. Place all of the ingredients in your blender, and blend until you get a creamy smoothie.

STRAWBERRY BLUEBERRY SMOOTHIE

Nutrition: Cal 142; Fat 3 g; Carb 28 g; Protein 4 g
Serving 1; Cook time 10 min

Ingredients
- 250 g (8.8oz) frozen raspberry and strawberries
- 3 bananas peeled
- 2 tbsp almond butter
- 240 ml (1 cup) cold nonfat milk
- 60 ml (0.25 cup) peach juice
- 2 tbsp maple syrup

Instructions
1. Place all of the ingredients in your blender, and blend until you get a creamy smoothie.

VEGAN PUMPKIN PIE SMOOTHIE

Nutrition: Cal 231; Fat 3 g; Carb 45 g; Protein 4 g
Serving 1; Cook time 10 min

Ingredients
- 1 frozen banana
- 1/2 avocado
- 1/2 cup frozen pumpkin purée
- 1/3 cup non-frozen pumpkin purée
- 3/4 cup plant milk (I used oat)
- 1/4 teaspoon vanilla
- 1 teaspoon pumpkin pie spice
- 1/2 teaspoon cinnamon
- 1,5 tablespoons maple syrup

Instructions
1. Place all of the ingredients in your blender, and blend until you get a creamy smoothie.

STONE FRUIT SMOOTHIE

Nutrition: Cal 142; Fat 3 g; Carb 28 g; Protein 4 g
Serving 1; Cook time 10 min

Ingredients
- 1 cup chopped plums
- 1 cup frozen cherries
- 1 banana sliced and frozen
- 1/4 cup apple juice
- 1 Tbsp honey can sub maple or agave
- 1/2 tsp cinnamon
- 1 Tbsp chia seeds optional

Instructions
1. Place all of the ingredients in your blender, and blend until you get a creamy smoothie.

SWEET POTATO SMOOTHIE

Nutrition: Cal 372; Fat 3 g; Carb 55 g; Protein 4 g
Serving 1; Cook time 10 min

Ingredients
- 1 small sweet potato baked, cut, and frozen (6.5 ounces/1 1/2 cups cubed)
- 1 cup frozen cauliflower rice (100 grams)
- 1 tablespoon almond butter
- 1/2 teaspoon vanilla extract
- 1/2 tablespoon cinnamon
- 1/4 teaspoon nutmeg
- 1 teaspoon maple syrup (optional)
- 1 1/2 cups unsweetened vanilla almond milk (or more or less depending on smoothie thickness preference)

Instructions
1. Place all of the ingredients in your blender, and blend until you get a creamy smoothie.

BERRY FENNEL SMOOTHIE

Nutrition: Cal 593; Fat 0 g; Carb 28 g; Protein 27 g
Serving 1; Cook time 10 min

Ingredients
- 1 apple cored and sliced
- 1 cup fennel slices
- 1 cup frozen berries
- 1-2 cups baby spinach leaves
- ½ cup plain yoghurt
- 1 cup oat milk or other non-dairy milk

Instructions
1. Place all of the ingredients in your blender, and blend until you get a creamy smoothie.

FENNEL FROND AND PINEAPPLE SMOOTHIE

Nutrition: Cal 191; Fat 3 g; Carb 47 g; Protein 6 g
Serving 1; Cook time 10 min

Ingredients
- 2 cups coconut water
- 1 cup loosely packed fennel fronds
- 2 cups frozen pineapple chunks
- 2 ripe bananas

Instructions
1. Place all of the ingredients in your blender, and blend until you get a creamy smoothie.

POMELO SMOOTHIE

Nutrition: Cal 568; Fat 3 g; Carb 142 g; Protein 4 g
Serving 1; Cook time 10 min

Ingredients
- 8.8 ounces Pomelo
- 2 Passion Fruits aka Maracuja
- Sapote aka Chikoo fruit
- 1/2 cup Coconut Milk

Instructions
1. Place all of the ingredients in your blender, and blend until you get a creamy smoothie.

BLUEBERRY SMOOTHIE

Nutrition: Cal 147; Fat 3 g; Carb 28 g; Protein 4 g
Serving 1; Cook time 10 min

Ingredients
- 1 cup frozen blueberries
- 1 cup frozen sliced bananas
- 1 tablespoon flax meal
- 1/2 –1 cup milk, any kind (we used unsweetened almond milk)
- 1 teaspoon vanilla extract

Instructions
1. Place all of the ingredients in your blender, and blend until you get a creamy smoothie.
2.

CARROT APPLE SMOOTHIE WITH GINGER

Nutrition: Cal 342; Fat 3 g; Carb 46 g; Protein 4 g
Serving 1; Cook time 10 min

Ingredients
- 2 medium carrots scrubbed and peeled if desired, cut into chunks
- large apple cored and sliced into quarters
- 1 tablespoon fresh ginger A chunk about the size of your thumb
- 1/2 1 lemon juiced
- tablespoon hemp seeds
- 1/2 teaspoon ground cinnamon
- 1 cup ice cubes
- 1 - 1 1/2 cups cold water

Instructions
1. Place all of the ingredients in your blender, and blend until you get a creamy smoothie.

EASY BERRY POMEGRANATE SMOOTHIE

Nutrition: Cal 145; Fat 3 g; Carb 36 g; Protein 4 g
Serving 1; Cook time 10 min

Ingredients
- 1/2 cup frozen mixed berries
- 1/2 cup pomegranate juice
- 1 banana
- 2 cups ice water

Instructions
1. Place all of the ingredients in your blender, and blend until you get a creamy smoothie.

TROPICAL JACKFRUIT SMOOTHIE

Nutrition: Cal 150; Fat 1 g; Carb 25 g; Protein 4 g
Serving 1; Cook time 10 min

Ingredients
- 7 pieces fresh jackfruit
- 1/4 cup frozen banana slices
- 1/2 cup frozen mango chunks
- 1/2 cup well shaken canned coconut milk, unsweetened
- 1/3 cup pineapple juice

Instructions

1. Place all of the ingredients in your blender, and blend until you get a creamy smoothie.

CREAMY APPLE STRAWBERRY SMOOTHIE

Nutrition: Cal 212; Fat 3 g; Carb 35 g; Protein 4 g
Serving 1; Cook time 10 min

Ingredients
- 1/2 cups strawberries about 10 large strawberries
- 1 banana peeled, fresh or frozen
- 1 apple fugi, gala, or any sweet apple chopped with skin on.
- 3 tablespoons heavy cream almond milk, soy milk, coconut milk, or dairy milk can be used.
- 1/2 cup ice cuber

Instructions
1. Place all of the ingredients in your blender, and blend until you get a creamy smoothie.

SIMPLE STRAWBERRY OAT MILK LACTATION SMOOTHIE

Nutrition: Cal 212; Fat 9 g; Carb 38 g; Protein 4 g
Serving 1; Cook time 10 min

Ingredients
- 10 Strawberries Cored
- 1/2 cup oat milk
- 1 banana peeled, fresh or frozen
- 1 Medjool Date pitted
- 1/4 cup oats rolled, old-fashioned
- tablespoons hemp seeds hemp hearts
- 1 cup ice cubes

Instructions
1. Place all of the ingredients in your blender, and blend until you get a creamy smoothie.

POST WORKOUT SMOOTHIE

Nutrition: Cal 198; Fat 3 g; Carb 26 g; Protein 4 g
Serving 1; Cook time 10 min

Ingredients
- 1 banana
- 1 cup chopped strawberries
- 1 cup plant milk of your choice we used oat milk
- 1 tbsp peanut butter

Instructions
1. Place all of the ingredients in your blender, and blend until you get a creamy smoothie.

EASY MANGO SMOOTHIE

Nutrition: Cal 412; Fat 3 g; Carb 28 g; Protein 4 g
Serving 1; Cook time 10 min

Ingredients
- 2 large mangoes (peeled, chopped & frozen)
- 1 cup coconut milk
- 1 cup almond milk
- 2 teaspoons honey
- 1 frozen banana

Instructions

1. Place all of the ingredients in your blender, and blend until you get a creamy smoothie.

ACTIVATED CHARCOAL SMOOTHIE

Nutrition: Cal 412; Fat 3 g; Carb 47 g; Protein 4 g
Serving 1; Cook time 10 min

Ingredients
- 1 banana (fresh or frozen)
- 1 tbsp chia seeds
- ½ cup mixed berries (fresh or frozen)
- 1 tbsp maple syrup (or agave syrup)
- 10 almonds
- 1 tsp activated charcoal powder
- Any desired toppings: such as fresh fruit, berries, a sprinkle of granola, chia seeds, coconut flakes, nuts, and/or seeds.

Instructions
1. Place all of the ingredients in your blender, and blend until you get a creamy smoothie.

KIWI BERRY SMOOTHIE

Nutrition: Cal 148; Fat 3 g; Carb 37 g; Protein 4 g
Serving 1; Cook time 10 min

Ingredients
- 1/2 cup Blueberries
- 1/2 cup Raspberries
- 1/2 fruit (2" dia) Kiwi fruit
- 1/2 medium (7" to 7-7/8" long) Banana

Instructions
1. Place all of the ingredients in your blender, and blend until you get a creamy smoothie.

BERRY YOGURT SMOOTHIE

Nutrition: Cal 202; Fat 3 g; Carb 28 g; Protein 4 g
Serving 1; Cook time 10 min

Ingredients
- 1 cup (8 fl oz) Nonfat yogurt
- 1/3 cup, sliced Banana
- 7 berry Strawberries

Instructions
1. Place all of the ingredients in your blender, and blend until you get a creamy smoothie.

BLACKBERRY ACTIVATED CHARCOAL SMOOTHIE

Nutrition: Cal 412; Fat 2 g; Carb 48 g; Protein 4 g
Serving 1; Cook time 10 min

Ingredients
- 1 cup frozen blackberries or mixed berries can be substituted
- 2 frozen bananas
- 1/4-1/3 cup plant-based milk i.e. almond
- 1 tablespoon activated charcoal
- 1 cup fresh spinach
- Toppings:
- 1 teaspoon hemp hearts optional
- 1/4 cup "raw-nola" optional see note
- 1/2 fresh banana sliced
- 1/4 cup blueberries

Instructions
1. Place all of the ingredients in your blender, and blend until you get a creamy smoothie.

CHIA BANANA BOOST SMOOTHIE

Nutrition: Cal 562; Fat 3 g; Carb 64 g; Protein 17 g
Serving 1; Cook time 10 min

Ingredients
- 1 banana frozen
- 2 tablespoons chia seeds
- 2 tablespoons peanut butter
- 2 tbsp oats
- 2 tbsp unsweetened coconut flakes
- 1 date pitted
- 1 teaspoon cinnamon
- 1 cup almond mil

Instructions
1. Place all of the ingredients in your blender, and blend until you get a creamy smoothie.

COPYCAT CARIBBEAN PASSION SMOOTHIE

Nutrition: Cal 342; Fat 3 g; Carb 80 g; Protein 4 g
Serving 1; Cook time 10 min

Ingredients
- 2 cups Orange Peach Mango juice
- 8 ounces frozen strawberries
- 6 ounces frozen peaches
- 3 large scoops orange sherbet

Instructions
1. Place all of the ingredients in your blender, and blend until you get a creamy smoothie.

PINEAPPLE SMOOTHIE

Nutrition: Cal 140; Fat 3 g; Carb 31 g; Protein 4 g
Serving 1; Cook time 10 min

Ingredients
- 1/2 pineapple, trimmed, peeled and chopped
- 1 small banana, peeled and sliced
- 1 lime, juiced
- ice (optional)

Instructions
1. Place all of the ingredients in your blender, and blend until you get a creamy smoothie.

RASPBERRY AND APPLE SMOOTHIE

Nutrition: Cal 106; Fat 3 g; Carb 28 g; Protein 4 g
Serving 1; Cook time 10 min

Ingredients
- 2 apples, cored (we used Granny Smith)
- 1/2 frozen raspberries
- 1/2 natural yogurt
- 2 tbsp porridge oats
- 1/2 lemon, juiced
- 1/2 milk

Instructions

1. Place all of the ingredients in your blender, and blend until you get a creamy smoothie.

STRAWBERRY KIWI SMOOTHIE

Nutrition: Cal 142; Fat 3 g; Carb 28 g; Protein 4 g
Serving 1; Cook time 10 min

Ingredients
- 2 cups frozen strawberries (16 oz bag)
- 2 tablespoons honey
- 1 teaspoon chia seeds
- 2 cups honey greek yogurt
- 1 kiwis, peels and sliced
- 1/2 cup water

Instructions
1. Place all of the ingredients in your blender, and blend until you get a creamy smoothie.

LOW CALORIE SMOOTHIES

Nutrition: Cal 87; Fat 2 g; Carb 10 g; Protein 4 g
Serving 1; Cook time 10 min

Ingredients
- 1 cup frozen strawberries
- 1/2 cup unsweetened almond milk

Instructions
1. Place all of the ingredients in your blender, and blend until you get a creamy smoothie.

AVOCADO & STRAWBERRY SMOOTHIE

Nutrition: Cal 192; Fat 11 g; Carb 15 g; Protein 4 g
Serving 1; Cook time 10 min

Ingredients
- 1/2 avocado, stoned, peeled and cut into chunks
- 1/2 cup g strawberry, halved
- 4 tbsp low-fat natural yogurt
- 200ml semi-skimmed milk
- lemon or lime juice, to taste
- honey, to taste

Instructions
1. Place all of the ingredients in your blender, and blend until you get a creamy smoothie.

KIWI FRUIT SMOOTHIE

Nutrition: Cal 163; Fat 1 g; Carb 38 g; Protein 4 g
Serving 1; Cook time 10 min

Ingredients
- 3 peeled kiwi fruit
- 1 mango, peeled, stoned and chopped
- 500ml pineapple juice
- 1 banana, sliced

Instructions
1. Place all of the ingredients in your blender, and blend until you get a creamy smoothie.

BANANA, CLEMENTINE & MANGO SMOOTHIE

Nutrition: Cal 142; Fat 3 g; Carb 28 g; Protein 4 g
Serving 1; Cook time 10 min

Ingredients
- about 24 juicy clementines, plus an extra one for decoration
- 2 small, very ripe and juicy mangoes
- 2 ripe bananas
- 500g tub whole milk or low-fat yogurt
- handful of ice cubes (optional)

Instructions
1. Place all of the ingredients in your blender, and blend until you get a creamy smoothie.

AVOCADO & BANANA SMOOTHIE

Nutrition: Cal 134; Fat 3 g; Carb 48 g; Protein 4 g
Serving 1; Cook time 10 min

Ingredients
- medium banana, sliced
- 1/2 avocado, pitted and sliced
- teaspoons honey
- 5-6 ice cubes
- 2/3 cup unsweetened vanilla coconut milk or almond milk

Instructions
1. Place all of the ingredients in your blender, and blend until you get a creamy smoothie.

COCONUT JOY VEGAN SMOOTHIE

Nutrition: Cal 359; Fat 3 g; Carb 51 g; Protein 4 g
Serving 1; Cook time 10 min

Ingredients
- 1 cup spinach
- ½ cup coconut milk
- 1 banana (frozen)
- 1 tablespoon almond butter
- 1 tablespoon cacao powder
- 1 tablespoon maple syrup

Instructions
1. Place all of the ingredients in your blender, and blend until you get a creamy smoothie.

BRAIN FOG CURE SMOOTHIE

Nutrition: Cal 112; Fat 3 g; Carb 28 g; Protein 4 g
Serving 1; Cook time 10 min

Ingredients
- C1 up spinach
- 1 cup green tea (brewed and chilled)
- 3/4 cups raspberries (frozen)
- 3/4 cups blueberries (frozen)

Instructions
1. Place all of the ingredients in your blender, and blend until you get a creamy smoothie.

RASPBERRY LEMON SMOOTHIE

Nutrition: Cal 418; Fat 3 g; Carb 45 g; Protein 4 g
Serving 1; Cook time 10 min

Ingredients
- 8 oz. lemon yogurt
- 1 cup coconut milk
- 1 cup frozen raspberries (or fresh)
- 1 tbl honey
- 1 cup crushed ice

Instructions
1. Place all of the ingredients in your blender, and blend until you get a creamy smoothie.

VEGAN RASPBERRY PEANUT BUTTER SMOOTHIE

Nutrition: Cal 270; Fat 13 g; Carb 38 g; Protein 4 g
Serving 1; Cook time 10 min

Ingredients
- 1/2 banana
- 1 cup raspberries
- 1 cup almond milk
- 1 tablespoon peanut butter
- 1/2 cup ice

Instructions
1. Place all of the ingredients in your blender, and blend until you get a creamy smoothie.

CHERRY COLLAGEN SMOOTHIE

Nutrition: Cal 92; Fat 3 g; Carb 22 g; Protein 4 g
Serving 1; Cook time 10 min

Ingredients
- 3/4 cup water
- 1/4 cup beets (peeled and diced, raw or cooked)
- 1 cup spinach (fresh)
- 3/4 cup cherries (frozen, pitted)
- 1 scoop collagen powder
- 1 tablespoon lemon (juice)

Instructions
1. Place all of the ingredients in your blender, and blend until you get a creamy smoothie.

SAUERKRAUT JUICE SMOOTHIE

Nutrition: Cal 172; Fat 3 g; Carb 48 g; Protein 4 g
Serving 1; Cook time 10 min

Ingredients
- 1 cup kombucha (ginger)
- 1 cup pineapple (frozen)
- ½ cup peach (frozen)
- 1 tablespoon raw sauerkraut juice (refrigerated)
- ½ inch ginger root

Instructions
1. Place all of the ingredients in your blender, and blend until you get a creamy smoothie.

ELECTROLYTE RECOVERY SMOOTHIE

Nutrition: Cal 452; Fat 3 g; Carb 21 g; Protein 4 g
Serving 1; Cook time 10 min

Ingredients
- cup unsweetened soy milk or protein oat milk
- tab effervescent recovery tabs
- ½ cup frozen strawberries
- ½ cup frozen mango or peaches

Instructions
1. Place all of the ingredients in your blender, and blend until you get a creamy smoothie.

PURPLE PASSION GREEN SMOOTHIE

Nutrition: Cal 282; Fat 0 g; Carb 28 g; Protein 4 g
Serving 1; Cook time 10 min

Ingredients
- ½ cup strawberries
- ¼ cup blueberries
- cup raw spinach
- ¼ cup Greek yogurt
- 1 cup water

Instructions
1. Place all of the ingredients in your blender, and blend until you get a creamy smoothie.

MOCHA SMOOTHIE WITH COCONUT MILK

Nutrition: Cal 157; Fat 3 g; Carb358 g; Protein 4 g
Serving 1; Cook time 10 min

Ingredients
- 1/3 cup brewed coffee chilled
- 1/3 cup unsweetened coconut milk
- 2 scoops Chocolate Protein Powder
- 1/2 cup ice

Instructions
1. Place all of the ingredients in your blender, and blend until you get a creamy smoothie.

PINEAPPLE COCONUT MILK SMOOTHIES

Nutrition: Cal 152; Fat 3 g; Carb 35 g; Protein 4 g
Serving 1; Cook time 10 min

Ingredients
- 1/4 cup 0% Greek Yogurt or cashew yogurt
- 1/3 cup unsweetened coconut milk
- 1/2 cup ice
- cup frozen pineapple
- 1 tablespoon oats optional

Instructions
1. Place all of the ingredients in your blender, and blend until you get a creamy smoothie.

HEALTHY MIXED BERRY SMOOTHIE

Nutrition: Cal 122; Fat 3 g; Carb 25 g; Protein 4 g
Serving 1; Cook time 10 min

Ingredients
- 1/2 cups unsweetened almond milk
- 2 cups mixed berries frozen (10 oz)
- banana frozen
- ½ tsp vanilla extract
- 1 TBS honey
- TBS vanilla protein powder optional
- 1 cup spinach optional

Instructions
1. Place all of the ingredients in your blender, and blend until you get a creamy smoothie.

PEANUT BUTTER BANANA COCONUT MILK SMOOTHIE

Nutrition: Cal 162; Fat 3 g; Carb 38 g; Protein 3 g
Serving 1; Cook time 10 min

Ingredients
- 1/2 cup unsweetened coconut milk
- 1/2 cup ice
- 1 tablespoon peanut butter
- 1 banana sliced and frozen

Instructions
1. Place all of the ingredients in your blender, and blend until you get a creamy smoothie.

STRAWBERRY COCONUT MILK SMOOTHIE

Nutrition: Cal 132; Fat 3 g; Carb 38 g; Protein 4 g
Serving 1; Cook time 10 min

Ingredients
- 1/4 cup 0% Greek Yogurt or cashew yogurt
- 1/3 cup unsweetened coconut milk
- 1/2 cup ice
- 1/2 cup strawberries fresh or frozen
- 1 tablespoon oats optional

Instructions
1. Place all of the ingredients in your blender, and blend until you get a creamy smoothie.

STRAWBERRY BANANA COCONUT MILK SMOOTHIE

Nutrition: Cal 145; Fat 3 g; Carb 38 g; Protein 4 g
Serving 1; Cook time 10 min

Ingredients
- banana sliced and frozen
- 1 cup strawberries
- 1/3 cup unsweetened coconut milk
- 1/2 cup ice
- 1 tablespoon oats optional

Instructions
1. Place all of the ingredients in your blender, and blend until you get a creamy smoothie.

CHOCOLATE CHERRY ANTI-INFLAMMATORY SMOOTHIE

Nutrition: Cal 149; Fat 3 g; Carb 30 g; Protein 4 g
Serving 1; Cook time 10 min

Ingredients
- 1 cup baby spinach
- 1 cup dark red cherries pitted (frozen is ideal)
- 1 tablespoon unsweetened cocoa powder

- 1 cup almond milk (or oat milk)

Instructions
1. Place all of the ingredients in your blender, and blend until you get a creamy smoothie.

MEAL REPLACEMENT SMOOTHIE FOR WEIGHT LOSS

Nutrition: Cal 192; Fat 3 g; Carb 30 g; Protein 4 g
Serving 1; Cook time 10 min

Ingredients
- 1 cup assorted frozen berry medley (strawberries, raspberries, blueberries)
- 1/2 cup baby spinach
- 1 tablespoon almond butter or your favorite nut butter
- 2 scoops Vanilla Protein Powder
- 1 tablespoon uncooked oatmeal or gluten free oatmeal
- 1 cup water and more to thin as needed/desired

Instructions
1. Place all of the ingredients in your blender, and blend until you get a creamy smoothie.

MIXED BERRY COCONUT MILK SMOOTHIES

Nutrition: Cal 152; Fat 3 g; Carb 35 g; Protein 4 g
Serving 1; Cook time 10 min

Ingredients
- 1/4 cup vanilla Greek Yogurt or cashew yogurt
- 1/3 cup unsweetened coconut milk
- 1/2 cup ice
- 2/3 cup frozen berry medley
- 1 tablespoon oats optional

Instructions
1. Place all of the ingredients in your blender, and blend until you get a creamy smoothie.

VANILLA PEACH COCONUT MILK SMOOTHIE

Nutrition: Cal 142; Fat 3 g; Carb 28 g; Protein 4 g
Serving 1; Cook time 10 min

Ingredients
- 1/4 cup vanilla Greek Yogurt or cashew yogurt
- 1/3 cup unsweetened coconut milk
- 1/2 cup ice
- 1 peach sliced
- 1 tablespoon oats optional

Instructions
1. Place all of the ingredients in your blender, and blend until you get a creamy smoothie.

LOW CARB SMOOTHIE

Nutrition: Cal 202; Fat 3 g; Carb 15 g; Protein 4 g
Serving 1; Cook time 10 min

Ingredients
1/2 cup mixed berries we used blueberries and blackberries
1/2 cup low fat cottage cheese
1/2 cup unsweetened almond milk

Instructions
1. Place all of the ingredients in your blender, and blend until you get a creamy smoothie.

LOW CALORIE PAPAYA SMOOTHIES

Nutrition: Cal 236; Fat 3 g; Carb 40 g; Protein 4 g
Serving 1; Cook time 10 min

Ingredients
- 1 cup papaya frozen or fresh
- 1/2 cup mango frozen or fresh
- 1/4 cup 0% Greek Yogurt
- 1/3 cup water and more to thin as needed/desired
- 1 scoop Prebiotic/Probiotic Powder optional
- 1 teaspoon honey optional

Instructions
1. Place all of the ingredients in your blender, and blend until you get a creamy smoothie.

WEIGHT LOSS COLLAGEN SMOOTHIE

Nutrition: Cal 202; Fat 3 g; Carb 28 g; Protein 4 g
Serving 1; Cook time 10 min

Ingredients
- 1/2 cup strawberries fresh or frozen
- 1/2 cup raspberries fresh or frozen
- 1/4 cup blueberries fresh or frozen
- Juice of one orange fresh is important, see intro
- 2 scoops Collagen Powder
- 1/2 cup water plus more as needed

Instructions
1. Place all of the ingredients in your blender, and blend until you get a creamy smoothie.

RED VELVET SMOOTHIE

Nutrition: Cal 162; Fat 3 g; Carb 48 g; Protein 4 g
Serving 1; Cook time 10 min

Ingredients
- 1 cup spinach
- 1 cup coconut milk
- 1 cup strawberries (frozen)
- medjool dates (pitted)
- 1 tablespoon beet (raw or cooked)
- 1 tablespoon cacao powder
- ½ teaspoon vanilla extract

Instructions
1. Place all of the ingredients in your blender, and blend until you get a creamy smoothie.

BERRY ORANGE SMOOTHIE

Nutrition: Cal 182; Fat 3 g; Carb 38 g; Protein 2 g
Serving 1; Cook time 10 min

Ingredients
- 1 cup frozen mixed berries
- 1/2 cup low-fat plain yogurt
- 1 teaspoon grated orange zest
- 1/4 cup freshly squeezed orange juice

Instructions
1. Place all of the ingredients in your blender, and blend until you get a creamy smoothie.

STRAWBERRY BANANA SMOOTHIE

<u>Nutrition: Cal 200; Fat 3 g; Carb 48 g; Protein 4 g
Serving 1; Cook time 10 min</u>
Ingredients
- (13.5 oz.) can of light coconut milk
- 1,5 cups sliced frozen strawberries
- 1 medium frozen chopped banana
- 1/4 cup rolled oats
- 1 tablespoon maple syrup

Instructions
1. Place all of the ingredients in your blender, and blend until you get a creamy smoothie.

BANANA BLUEBERRY AND SPINACH SMOOTHIE

<u>Nutrition: Cal 270 ; Fat 3 g; Carb 5 g; Protein 4 g
Serving 1; Cook time 10 min</u>
Ingredients
- 1 banana
- 1 cup blueberries fresh or frozen
- 1 cup baby spinach
- 1/2 cup water
- 1 scoop Vanilla Protein Powder

Instructions
1. Place all of the ingredients in your blender, and blend until you get a creamy smoothie.

OCEAN SMOOTHIE

<u>Nutrition: Cal 200; Fat 3 g; Carb 58 g; Protein 4 g
Serving 1; Cook time 10 min</u>
Ingredients
- 1 cup frozen banana
- 1 cup frozen mango chunks
- ¼ teaspoon blue spirulina
- ¼ teaspoon green spirulina
- splash milk of choice if needed

Instructions
1. Place all of the ingredients in your blender, and blend until you get a creamy smoothie.

ULTIMATE BANANA NICE CREAM

<u>Nutrition: Cal 115; Fat 1 g; Carb 27 g; Protein 4 g
Serving 1; Cook time 10 min</u>
Ingredients
- 4 bananas (peeled sliced and frozen)
- ¼ cup coconut milk
- dash blue spirulina

Instructions
1. Place all of the ingredients in your blender, and blend until you get a creamy smoothie.

BANANA, HONEY & HAZELNUT SMOOTHIE

<u>Nutrition: Cal 230; Fat 3 g; Carb 37 g; Protein 4 g
Serving 1; Cook time 10 min</u>
Ingredients
- peeled, sliced banana
- 250ml soya milk
- 1 tsp honey
- a little grated nutmeg
- 1 tsp chopped hazelnuts , to serve

Instructions
1. Place all of the ingredients in your blender, and blend until you get a creamy smoothie.

ANTI-CANCER GREEN SMOOTHIE

<u>Nutrition: Cal 202; Fat 10 g; Carb 24 g; Protein 8g
Serving 1; Cook time 10 min</u>
Ingredients
- 1/4 cup hemp seeds
- 2 cups carrot juice
- 1 cup water
- 1 ripe banana, frozen
- 1 cup frozen strawberries
- 1 cup frozen broccoli florets
- 2 cups fresh or lightly steamed baby kale or baby spinach
- 5 fresh mint leaves
- 1,5 tablespoons cocoa powder
- 1/2 lime or lemon, juiced

Instructions
1. Place all of the ingredients in your blender, and blend until you get a creamy smoothie.

OAT MILK SMOOTHIE WITH STRAWBERRY AND BANANA

<u>Nutrition: Cal 180; Fat 3 g; Carb 40 g; Protein 2 g
Serving 1; Cook time 10 min</u>
Ingredients
- 2 cups homemade oat milk or boxed oat milk
- frozen ripe banana, broken in half
- 1 cup frozen strawberries
- tablespoons almond butter or peanut butter
- scoops unsweetened protein powder (optional, for added nutrition)

Instructions
1. Place all of the ingredients in your blender, and blend until you get a creamy smoothie.

PEANUT BUTTER SMOOTHIE

<u>Nutrition: Cal 167; Fat 3 g; Carb 30 g; Protein 4 g
Serving 1; Cook time 10 min</u>
Ingredients
- 1 cup oat milk
- 1 banana, peeled and chopped
- 1/2 cup peanut butter
- 1 tbsp rolled oats
- pinch of cinnamon
- pinch of allspice
- pinch of nutmeg (optional)
- small handful ice cubes

Instructions
1. Place all of the ingredients in your blender, and blend until you get a creamy smoothie.

BLACKBERRY SMOOTHIE

Nutrition: Cal 316; Fat 3 g; Carb 53 g; Protein 15 g
Serving 1; Cook time 10 min

Ingredients
- 1 cup fresh blackberries (6 ounces)
- 1/2 medium banana
- 1/2 cup plain whole-milk Greek yogurt
- 1 tablespoon honey
- 1/2 teaspoons fresh lemon juice
- 1 teaspoon finely chopped fresh ginger

Instructions
1. Place all of the ingredients in your blender, and blend until you get a creamy smoothie.

MORINGA SMOOTHIE

Nutrition: Cal 251; Fat 3 g; Carb 41 g; Protein 4 g
Serving 1; Cook time 10 min

Ingredients
- 1 cup unsweetened almond milk (or your favorite plant milk)
- 1/2 cup fresh moringa leaves (or 2 teaspoons moringa powder)
- 1 frozen banana, broken into chunks
- 1/2 cup frozen pineapple
- 1 tablespoon hemp seeds

Instructions
1. Place all of the ingredients in your blender, and blend until you get a creamy smoothie.

AVOCADO CHOCOLATE SMOOTHIE (VEGAN)

Nutrition: Cal 170; Fat 3 g; Carb 48 g; Protein 2 g
Serving 1; Cook time 10 min

Ingredients
- 2 cups unsweetened almond milk (or your choice of milk)
- 2 tablespoons maple syrup
- 1/2 ripe avocado, with the peel and pit removed
- 1 frozen banana, broken in half
- 1,5 tablespoons cocoa powder
- 1/2 teaspoon vanilla extract
- 1 cup ice (optional, if you prefer a thicker smoothie)

Instructions
1. Place all of the ingredients in your blender, and blend until you get a creamy smoothie.

ZUCCHINI STRAWBERRY SMOOTHIE

Nutrition: Cal 293; Fat 3 g; Carb 51 g; Protein 4 g
Serving 1; Cook time 10 min

Ingredients
- 1 cup unsweetened almond milk
- 1 cup frozen strawberries
- 1 cup frozen sliced zucchini
- 2 tablespoons peanut butter or almond butter
- pitted dates

Instructions
1. Place all of the ingredients in your blender, and blend until you get a creamy smoothie.

VEGAN STRAWBERRY CHEESECAKE SMOOTHIE

Nutrition: Cal 341; Fat 12 g; Carb 42 g; Protein 6 g
Serving 1; Cook time 10 min

Ingredients
- 1/4 cup cashews, soaked in very hot water for 15 minutes, then rinsed and drained
- 1 cup unsweetened plant milk, I like oat milk or almond milk
- 1 1/4 cup frozen strawberries
- 1 frozen banana, broken into chunks
- 1/2 lemon, juiced
- 1 teaspoon vanilla extract
- 4 gluten-free wafer cookies, crushed (optional, for topping)

Instructions
1. Place all of the ingredients in your blender, and blend until you get a creamy smoothie.

MANGO STRAWBERRY BANANA SMOOTHIE

Nutrition: Cal 256; Fat 3 g; Carb 35 g; Protein 4 g
Serving 1; Cook time 10 min

Ingredients
- 1 cup orange juice
- 1/2 cup water
- 1 ripe banana, broken into chunks
- 1 cup frozen mango chunks
- 1/2 cup frozen strawberries

Instructions
1. Place all of the ingredients in your blender, and blend until you get a creamy smoothie.

PEANUT BUTTER CAULIFLOWER SMOOTHIE

Nutrition: Cal 250; Fat 3 g; Carb 38 g; Protein 4 g
Serving 1; Cook time 10 min

Ingredients
- 1 cup unsweetened almond milk
- 1 cup frozen cauliflower florets
- 1 frozen banana
- 2 tablespoons natural peanut butter
- 1/2 teaspoon vanilla extract
- Medjool dates

Instructions
1. Place all of the ingredients in your blender, and blend until you get a creamy smoothie.

STRAWBERRY BEET CONSTIPATION SMOOTHIE

Nutrition: Cal 156; Fat 13 g; Carb 22 g; Protein 43g
Serving 1; Cook time 10 min

Ingredients
- 1 cup unsweetened almond milk (you can use regular milk if you aren't on a dairy-free diet)
- 1 cup frozen strawberries
- 1 medium cooked beet, cut in half (see notes)
- 2 tablespoons chia seeds or 2 tablespoons ground flax
- 2 prunes
- 1/2-inch piece of fresh peeled ginger

Instructions

1. Place all of the ingredients in your blender, and blend until you get a creamy smoothie.

HONEYDEW SMOOTHIE

Nutrition: Cal 215; Fat 3 g; Carb 29 g; Protein 4 g
Serving 1; Cook time 10 min

Ingredients
- 1/2 cups of chopped honeydew (from about 1/2 of a honeydew melon)
- 1 cup chopped cucumber (from about 1 medium cucumber)
- 1/2 cup coconut milk
- 2–4 fresh mint leaves
- 1/2 cup crushed ice

Instructions
1. Place all of the ingredients in your blender, and blend until you get a creamy smoothie.

SWISS CHARD SMOOTHIE

Nutrition: Cal 206; Fat 3 g; Carb 38 g; Protein 4 g
Serving 1; Cook time 10 min

Ingredients
- 1/2 cups filtered water
- 2 tablespoons hemp seeds
- 1/2 frozen banana
- 1/4 cups frozen strawberries
- tablespoons peanut butter (or your choice of nut or seed butter)
- 2 large handfuls of Swiss chard (the leaves from one bunch)
- 2 scoops protein powder of your choice

Instructions

1. Place all of the ingredients in your blender, and blend until you get a creamy smoothie.

Berry Smoothie

Nutrition: Cal 221; Fat 3 g; Carb 52 g; Protein 4 g
Serving 1; Cook time 10 min

Ingredients
- 1/2 cups apple juice can also use almond milk, skim milk, coconut milk or other flavor of juice
- 1 banana sliced
- 1/2 cups frozen mixed berries
- 3/4 cup vanilla Greek yogurt
- 1 tablespoon honey optional

Instructions
1. Place all of the ingredients in your blender, and blend until you get a creamy smoothie.

FROZEN FRUIT SMOOTHIE

Nutrition: Cal 201; Fat 3 g; Carb 36 g; Protein 4 g
Serving 1; Cook time 10 min

Ingredients
- 1/2 cups apple juice
- 2 cups assorted frozen fruit I used cherries, raspberries, blueberries and mango
- 3/4 cup vanilla Greek yogurt
- additional fruit and/or mint sprigs for garnish optional

Instructions
1. Place all of the ingredients in your blender, and blend until you get a creamy smoothie.

Anthony Green

2022

Printed in Great Britain
by Amazon